THE BIKE WHISPERER

Changing the World
One Bike Rider at a Time

RICHARD E. KLEIN, PhD

DUMB
DICKIE
PRESS.

Published by Dumb Dickie Press

ISBN-13: 979-8-6296-3669-4
ISBN-10: 8-6296-3669-4

The Dumb Dickie Press logo is a trademark of Richard E. Klein.

Cover design by Ellen Meyer and Vicki Lesage

TABLE OF CONTENTS

INTRODUCTION

WHEN A CHILD masters riding and balancing on a two-wheeler, the child and his/her world has been transformed. Nothing is the same. The freedom now obtained is hard to even express or quantify. Clearly, mastery of the common two-wheeler represents a rite of passage—something that few other passages can come up to matching.

Unfortunately and seldom acknowledged, not every child attains mastery of two-wheelers. The discouragement and shame associated with defeat commonly cause a retreat from public recognition of the child's defeat. The child grows into adulthood burdened by the shame of being lesser to his/her bike riding peers.

For children with disabilities, public acceptance of a lesser status is recognized—recognized by a cadre of adults, the community, and even the child.

This is where I forced myself, uninvited, onto the scene. I, Richard E. Klein, although with no plan caused the world of bicycle instruction to be turned topsy-turvy. This book tells my story. The story is long, twisted, and arduous. But the story is worth the read—the journey as well as the ending are inspirational and uplifting. Welcome aboard. The ride is about to begin.

Albert Einstein said that a person should be pleased to have come up with even just one new idea in one's lifetime. I feel blessed. In my lifetime, I have come up with about half a dozen new creations. This book tells the story of one of those ideas.

Starting in 2001, I developed an adaptive bicycling instruction program. The program's thrust was to permit children with various disabilities, primarily Down syndrome, cerebral palsy, or autism spectrum disorder (ASD), to master riding two-wheelers. The program was built upon the idea that a series of trainer bikes will permit children to incrementally progress and thereby acquire the proper motor plans that lead to mastery of bike riding. To date, tens of thousands of children and their families have benefited.

Over the ensuing years, I have received inquiries that boil down to two questions. The first question is, "How did you come up with the idea of the program?" The second question, which typically follows in rapid succession, is, "Did you do this because you have a child with a disability?"

I can answer the second question quickly, with a simple "No." Most people who ask the first question expect a 30-second answer. In truth, there may be a short answer, but I haven't found it yet. Perhaps I could say that God planted the idea. However, in this book I will attempt to provide an answer in human terms. Ironically, after all is said and done, saying that God did it comes pretty close to being the best explanation. Of course, even God's hand in creating things can be elaborated on.

As the story unfolds, the time scale approaches a lifespan. The adaptive bike program came about largely because of many coincidences and accidental happenings, spanning the better part of my productive life. But one constant underlies the events: As the program evolved, I remained steadfast in pursuing a nebulous, ill-defined dream.

The origins of the adaptive bike program are deeply intertwined with my upbringing, education, formative years, and professional struggles. My early years and upbringing prepared me as a seed bed is prepared, and so I have woven many aspects of my life into the story.

The adaptive bike program came about only because of obstacles that faced me when I initially ventured in other professional directions. During my early life as a professor, my research focused on other areas, including:

- The prevention of skyscrapers from excessively swaying due to wind loads or earthquakes
- Exploring the perplexing question as to why the Earth has experienced periodic ice ages or glaciations

The details of my professional work in these two areas are treated in other writings. (See *The Deadly Gamble: A Post-Mortem of the World Trade Center Collapse* [1] for an overview of my research involvement in civil engineering structures.) I will merely say that I hit roadblocks in both endeavors.

The first roadblock came about because other professions, notably civil engineers, claimed domain over the design and construction of skyscrapers. Quite frankly, civil engineers have little interest in hearing how things might be done differently.

The second roadblock resulted from the shift of climate change discussions into hot button political topics. Whatever actual science might have once existed in this arena has been replaced with dark-age hysteria, largely by people with political agendas.

I suppose that being egotistical is something that goes hand-in-hand with being an inventor. The drive to build a better mouse trap inherently stems from an inventor's inner belief that he or she can do it better than anyone else. I recall a quotation that bears on this: "… but like all inventors, every goose to him represents a swan" from *In the Days of Bicycles and Bustles* [2]. I accept the reality that inventors tend to overestimate the worth of their invention. But again, that comes with the territory. If the inventor wasn't infatuated with an idea, it would never have become an invention in the first place.

RICHARD E. KLEIN, BIKE WHISPERER

FOR A RICHER UNDERSTANDING of the adaptive bike program, let's start at the beginning. What follows is my story, a truly personal story. It is laid out in a somewhat chronological order of how the program came to be.

The Driving Spark

IN MY ARCHIVES containing thousands of photographs, there is one that speaks volumes. The photograph is of a boy standing beside his bike in La Crosse, Wisconsin, in approximately the year 2000.

The boy, then about age 10, had been provided with a bike that had large outriggers. It appears, based on my clinical experience, that the boy had a diagnosis of mild cerebral palsy. A host of well-intentioned persons made the collective decision that this boy *needed* such a contraption because riding a conventional bike wasn't a possibility for him.

The people responsible for this conclusion likely included the parents, the pediatrician, the bicycle shop employee, the boy's school teacher, and possibly a therapist or two. Even the boy himself accepted the consensus decree, as these kids are quite amazing in their ability to accept the cards dealt to them. All involved persons acted as a unified force that came up with a unified decision. I can assure you that a boy or girl such as this might ride this contraption for a while, but after being the target of ridicule and derision, the child's desire to ride would soon ebb.

These types of kids typically go through three phases related to biking.

Once they try and fail, they conclude that they just aren't capable of riding a bike. In their mindset, riding a bike is impossible.

The second phase is the mindset, "I don't like biking." This phase reinforces their discouragement, so it becomes harder to get them to even try.

The third phase becomes the hardest nut to crack when they say, "I hate biking." Once this phase is reached, the child has decided once and for all that they will never get on a bike again. The task of teaching a skill like biking to somebody who doesn't want to learn is nothing short of gargantuan.

In the case of this boy in La Crosse, I'm pleased to report that he attended one of our early camps. Within a few short hours after being on my adaptive training bikes, those cumbersome and stigma-prone training wheels were removed, and he mastered riding that very same bike as a two-wheeler.

I stood for many years as a lone dissenter against the hordes of professionals who prescribe training wheels and similar contraptions. In many cases, the prescription was flat-out wrong. Just look at my success story with the boy from La Crosse—he didn't need those embarrassing training wheels, he needed proper training.

For over three decades, virtually all my focus was dedicated to a single goal: to permit children and adults with special needs to master bike riding. I want children, like the boy from La Crosse, to enjoy the thrill of discovering how to ride a bike. I want them to experience the joy of feeling the wind in their faces.

The fundamental tools at my disposal included a series of specially designed bikes, starting with what I call the roller bike. I custom-made each of those special bikes. I did this work in my shop in Alton, Illinois. I was my only employee and did all the work myself, so I wore many hats: owner, worker, designer, banker, and janitor.

Above is a photograph of another child in the adaptive bike program. Her objective, as well as ours, was to master bike riding. The bike she is riding has a roller in the rear to tame the tipsiness. In a significant percentage of cases, the program and child achieve success. These kids frequently master bike riding quickly—often measured in hours.

My Childhood and Early Education (1939–1957)

1939-1945. I was born in 1939, the tail-end of the great depression of the 1930s. Economics of health care were different back then. While cleaning out my mother's home after her passing in 2002, I was surprised to find the receipt for her hospital stay when I was born. It's hard for people today to grasp just how much the value of a dollar has changed.

The bill for an entire week in the hospital in 1939 for my mother and me after my birth came to $24.25. Note that my father wasn't able to pay the bill in full. He was short by $6.50.

I grew up in a modest, blue-collar neighborhood in Stratford, Connecticut. Times were hard for many. The father's ability to provide "three squares and a roof" meant his ability to provide for his family. The phraseology "three squares" was common language back then referring to three square meals each day. This implied adequate food as opposed to starving or standing in a soup kitchen line. Back then, welfare checks and food stamps were unheard of. I can recall neighboring families that couldn't afford a telephone, a refrigerator, or even a car. At times, the cupboard, like Mother Hubbard's cupboard, was bare, with hardly a bone for the dog. One neighboring family didn't even have an indoor flush toilet but rather used an outhouse. But things weren't all bad, as that outhouse was big enough to be a two-holer.

My father had a steady job as a machinist for Bullard Machine Tool Company in Bridgeport, Connecticut. The photograph below shows my father's identification work badge *circa* World War II.

To my benefit, my father had accumulated a modest array of

machine tools in our basement. As a kid, I had access to tools like a South Bend engine lathe and a floor-standing drill press. I became comfortable working with metals and building things in general.

Because of the national mobilization during WWII, my father worked long hours. He worked all night in the graveyard shift, then upon arriving back home in the wee hours of the morning, he ate some food and went to bed. My mother's instructions for my brothers and me boiled down to:

1. "Don't be in the house. You kids are making too much noise. Your father is sleeping."

2. "Don't play in the yard. You're making too much noise. Go somewhere else. Your father is sleeping."

3. "When you hear the evening six o'clock whistle blow (at the power plant across the river, which could be heard a mile or more away), you have 10 minutes to get home. We eat dinner at 6:10 p.m." I should note that my father was not a patient man, especially at dinner time.

4. My mother never articulated this statement, but as I look back it was pretty clear: "Don't come home (before meal times) unless you're bleeding." Oh, and that meant bleeding badly.

Growing up, I enjoyed freedoms that my grandkids today can't even imagine. I lived in a world controlled by kids. As we played war games with wooden rifles that shot pretend bullets, we would shoot the opposing bad guy, "Bang, bang! You're dead." Often the reply came back, "Oh, no, I'm not! You missed."

1945-1946. In those days one didn't learn to ride a bike until one's legs were long enough to reach the pedals. I can recall a neighboring kid who used a bike with wooden blocks taped to the pedals so that his feet could reach them. The smallest bike size normally available had a 24-inch tire diameter.

Bikes were utilitarian and somewhat scarce. During WWII, bike production and sales were not national priorities. Metals and available machine shops were mostly used for war-related purposes. Older bikes were often recycled with patriotic fervor in scrap metal drives to be melted down to become raw material for war armaments. Although the end of WWII signaled better times, the better times didn't happen overnight. It took several years for our national economy to adjust to peacetime and the availability of consumer goods—including bicycles, particularly bikes as toys for kids.

1947. My father purchased a used 24-inch bike for me from a neighbor. I recall the little stucco house where we went to buy that dusty bike. The bike was in the neighbor's garage, leaning against a wall. The garage floor was dirt, something quite common in those days. The bike was so old that it had wooden rims, typical of bikes dating from the 1920s or earlier. It was originally painted red, but with age it had turned to a dull rusty color.

My father paid $6 for the bike. I can still remember him counting out the money bill by bill with a firm voice, "One buck, two bucks…" Having a buck or two in the wallet was the sign of a real man—a wealthy man.

I don't remember, but my father must have then pumped up the tires and lubricated the chain. What I do recall as if it was just yesterday (even though it was more than 70 years ago) is him placing me on the bike and pushing me down the incline on our street. I crashed on the first attempt. On the second try, I managed to stay upright, balancing by steering, albeit haphazardly. Few words were spoken. If I was hurt on that first fall, I knew that crying wasn't acceptable. My father had a distinct disdain for crybabies and wimps.

In the days and weeks that followed, I rode whenever I could. At first, my feet couldn't reach the ground, so I used the first step of our front porch to hop on and get myself started. As I went through my grade school years, my bicycle became an integral part of my life.

The photograph below shows our house at 235 Reed Street in Stratford, Connecticut, *circa* 1949.

1955. In my junior year of high school, I took on a part-time job after school working in a gas station. Back then, self-service stations didn't exist, so my job consisted of pumping gas and soon included servicing cars for customers. My starting pay was 75 cents per hour. By the time spring of '56 came, I bought my first car—a 1936 four-door Plymouth—for a whopping $10.

The above photograph is one of the few I still have of my first car. With me are some of my high school buddies. From left to right are Paul Shirra, LeRoy Cebik, myself, and Freddie Ashcroft.

My next car was a 1946 Ford business coupe, which cost me $75. Cars became my thing, and working on cars even more so. It wasn't until about 15 years later (in 1970) that I got back into bicycles.

1956. While in my junior year of high school, I joined the United States Army in the Enlisted Reserve Program. I had turned 17 a few months prior, so I needed a parental permission signature. America was engaged in the dark years of the Cold War where we were pitted against the Soviets. Our national defense was predicated on the concept of maintaining a large reserve force. Being trained, that force could be activated and sent into combat anywhere and on short notice.

All able-bodied males were required to serve in some capacity in the military. Two options were a six-year commitment that included two years of active duty or an eight-year commitment that included six months of active duty. Other options existed, such as Officer Candidate School (OCS) and even ROTC for those going the college route.

In the below photograph, taken in the summer of 1957, I'm preparing to leave for Camp Drum in upper New York State. I was 18 at the time.

I wanted two things: to get the clock started and to get it finished. Should a war break out during my enlistment, I understood that as a reservist I could be called up. Becoming an officer had no appeal because once one is a commissioned officer, the commission lasts a lifetime. I was offered the chance to go to OCS but turned it down. Instead, I went for the first option of enlisting in the reserve for six years. On paper I was enlisted from May 1956 through May 1962. My enlistment was later extended due to a crisis with the Soviets in the early 1960s.

Being from a working class neighborhood and having parents with no college education, the idea of going to college had never entered my mind. Although my father graduated from high school, my mother dropped out of school in the ninth grade. She became an apprentice in a sewing shop, paying some lady to teach her the trade of being a seamstress. As an apprentice in the 1930s, two years went by before she earned any money.

In my family, the things that mattered were getting a job and being humble. I recall once remarking about how something I had done was pretty good. That resulted in a terse reprimand from my mother about the sins that come with pride. My parents' attitude was to get a job and make a buck, even if the job was just sweeping floors.

The idea of becoming a professor with a PhD was something I would have never dreamed of. I never envisioned going to college. My part-time job at the local Sunoco gas station soon expanded to 40 hours per week. I worked after school four hours each school day from Monday to Friday and then 10 hours on both Saturday and Sunday. Most people would call that a full-time job.

Obviously, my grades suffered. I did as little as possible and neglected to turn in most homework assignments. When a pupil fails to turn in homework assignments but can pass the exams, the typical course grade received is C. I didn't have to do homework or take exams in Band and P.E. Aside from the A grades in those two subjects, most of my other grades were significantly lower.

When I graduated from high school in 1957, my cumulative grades were so low that I stood just slightly above the mid-point in my class, ranking in the 59th percentile. I can assure my reader that even back in those days, grades that low wouldn't gain many acceptance letters from colleges. Most colleges selected students in the top five, ten, or possibly twenty percent. I was lightyears away from meeting that mark.

In addition, the guidance counselor at my high school, a stuffy old lady named Miss Ruth Cunningham, aimed only to groom kids for acceptance to prestigious Ivy League schools. I was told unequivocally that to be eligible to gain admission to college I would have to take two years of high school Latin and two years of a second foreign language, either French or Italian.

I survived my first year of Latin in the ninth grade, but by the next year I was flunking Latin II. Reciting Latin verb conjugations just didn't warm me up and I was allowed to drop the Latin course in my sophomore year. My refusal to learn Latin sealed my conviction that going to college was not in my future. The fact that I failed English the first semester of my junior year (note the report card above) shows that I was consistent in my dislike of language classes in almost any form. Like many young people, I didn't worry about the future. I assumed that I would eventually open a car repair business. In that profession, one certainly doesn't need to show anybody a report card.

In the fall of 1956, I started my senior year of high school. I also attended the army reserve weekly drills. And of course, I was still working 40 hours a week. It was then that President Dwight D. Eisenhower issued an executive order that impacted my life and my future. I don't understand his underlying motivation, but it occurred during Eisenhower's 1956 re-election bid, so politics may have played a role. Eisenhower's executive order was that active members of the reserves in good standing were no longer classified as 1-A and would no longer be first in line for the draft. Reservists were placed way down on the list. This was an unexpected boon for me. Because of the wording of my enlistment, I was never required to go on to the two years of active duty.

Because the draft was no longer an issue for me, I started thinking about college. My church, Our Savior's Danish Lutheran Church, supported Grandview College, a small two-year college in Des Moines, Iowa. In Danish tradition, it was akin to a school for the commoner class. Grandview "Junior" College was like an extension of high school.

The cost to attend Grandview College was within my family's budget, which was aided by a modest inheritance of about $3,000 from my mother's Danish parents. My mother and father decided that each of their three sons could attend college for one year using those funds. The cost for one year at Grandview was about $1,000.

Grandview College had low admission requirements. Basically, one had to be in the upper half of one's high school class. My 59th percentile barely met that requirement—but it did meet the requirement. Miss Cunningham's absurd dictate that one needed to have two years in each of two foreign languages was proven to be a myth. Of course, Grandview wasn't an Ivy League school, but I didn't care. In the absence of any other plan for my life, I applied to Grandview College and was accepted. I entered as a pre-engineering student. I reasoned that I had already bruised enough knuckles with wrenches slipping off nuts and bolts, so I decided on an engineering major. My goal was to design cars as opposed to repairing cars that somebody else had designed.

I served as a reservist for a total of seven years. For the last year, 1963, I had been placed on inactive reserve status, mostly due to fiscal reasons. Consequently, I was no longer required to go to summer camps and attend weekly drills. Federal funds must have been short as the available national defense budget was being redirected to the hostilities in Vietnam.

The idea of going to Vietnam was becoming increasingly unpopular. As Vietnam deployments ramped up, enlisting in the reserves or the National Guard became a trendy means of avoiding the draft, and the available slots became scarce. My earlier decision to enlist while in high school proved to be a blessing.

Another factor that helped me along in my reserve enlistment stemmed from a church connection. The officer who headed up the Army Reserve Center in Bridgeport, Captain Joseph Ugro, attended our church and was a close family friend. I didn't fully grasp the favors and protection being extended to me at the time, but I got assigned to a neat unit with easy duty. I received promotions as fast as I became eligible. People in high places were watching out for me. Within a year or two I had advanced to the rank of Specialist E-4, equivalent in pay grade to the rank of corporal. In contrast, I had numerous classmates who ended up being drafted and sent to Vietnam.

The College Years (1957–1968)

1957. I enrolled as a freshman at Grandview College in Des Moines, Iowa. Because Grandview was a Lutheran school, I received a modest scholarship as a Lutheran church member. My lackluster high school grades didn't matter.

I was greatly relieved to be out of the dreariness of the East Coast. Much of my disenfranchisement with Connecticut was rooted in gang-related violence. During my high school years, especially my sophomore year, I had been targeted by unsavory types, wannabe tough guys from the other side of town. They wore black leather jackets, had greased down "D.A." (duck ass) haircuts, and sported switch blade knives as their form of posturing. They never amounted to much either then or now, but nonetheless I had to deal with them. Once in Iowa, I also found relief in getting away from a torrid high school romance that had gone sour. Being at Grandview for me was like being in heaven. I did well in my classes. I didn't have to go to work 40 hours each week.

I drove the 20+ hours from Connecticut to Iowa nonstop, feeling considerable joy as I crossed the Mississippi River and went through Davenport. On U.S. Highway 6 heading west out of Davenport, I saw something truly unbelievable. The posted speed limit read simply, "Reasonable and Proper." There was no daytime speed limit!

The reverberations of my '46 Ford coupe, with its glass-pack mufflers and triple Stromberg carburetors on the Mercury V-8 engine, chilled my bones as I cruised along, often hitting speeds of 100+ MPH. The photograph below shows me standing beside my '46 Ford coupe in the snows of Iowa during the winter of 1957-58.

Above is another photograph. Note the Moonie wheel covers

and the '49 Mercury grill that I had installed.

Then, on October 4, 1957, the Soviet Union placed the first artificial satellite into Earth's orbit. In Russian, "Sputnik" translates to traveler or wanderer.

Sputnik, as per the above artist's sketch from the Internet, was relatively small compared to later satellites, weighing only 184 pounds. Sputnik's orbit wasn't precise, so after circling Earth for about three months, it was consumed by the atmosphere. The two things it did were transmit a beeping signal and scare the daylights out of our western smugness.

Because I was a new freshman enrolled in a pre-engineering program at the time of Sputnik's launch, I became swept up with so many other Americans to "catch up with the Russians." Americans as a whole were astonished to find that such a backward country could have beaten America into space. Sputnik's unexpected launch was the start of what became known as the post-Sputnik era in America (1957-1969). That intense era featured massive efforts in proving that America was still top dog. In 1961, President John F. Kennedy added to the intensity by proclaiming that by the end of the 1960s Americans would land a man on the moon and return him safely to Earth.

Without question, the launching of Sputnik dramatically changed the direction of my life. As I reflect back, I consider myself to be a product of this era. It's interesting to note that I concluded my education upon getting my PhD in 1968—closely coinciding with the successful Apollo lunar landing in the summer of 1969.

On the day of Sputnik's launch, I had been attending classes for about three weeks. Suddenly, my professors piled on homework in my science and math classes. America went into a panic. To think that the Soviets had done something the Americans couldn't was the equivalent of a national disgrace. To add to that disgrace, the U.S. Air Force soon after attempted launches that were televised live. Two attempts crashed with the entire nation watching. It wasn't until January 31, 1958 that the U.S. Navy succeeded in placing the first American satellite, Explorer I, into Earth's orbit.

In the fall of 1957, the Soviet's first satellite passed over the heartland of America, roughly every 96 minutes. We, as a nation and as a people, could do nothing about it. American fears intensified as the Soviets had "the bomb." If the satellite could go "beep-beep," it might also go "boom," or so the public mindset went. The race to reach the moon before the Russians became the focus of our society and our scientists.

The early 1960s. During my college years, I attended four different colleges and universities: Grandview College in Des Moines; the University of Iowa in Iowa City; Pennsylvania State University in University Park, Pennsylvania; and lastly Purdue University in West Lafayette, Indiana. For each transition, my ability to gain admission was dubious at best. I would make the cutoff each time, either from recent grades or passing a standardized test, although just barely.

One situation concerns a course called Ordinary Differential Equations, commonly called ODE or DEQ. That course was a brick wall that I had extreme difficulty getting past. I did so poorly most times—three times, in fact—that I dropped the course just before the drop date cut-off. On the fourth try, it was do or die. I was in a large section at Penn State. I didn't know one professor from another, but I happened to get a professor with the nickname Santa Claus, or so I found out later. His actual name was Professor Rodgers. I liked his style. He didn't lecture. Instead, he had students do homework problems on the blackboard. There was no pressure as he always got volunteers. The students at the blackboard described how they had solved the problem.

At the end of the semester, Professor Rodgers told his graduate graders to give 70 percent of the students A grades and the other 30 percent B grades. I was in the bottom third of his class. In those days, a grade of C was considered average. I received a grade of B, which in most circles was outstanding. In the world of mathematics, most A grades were reserved for the math majors rather than engineers. I would have felt lucky to have even passed that long-dreaded course with a D. Not only did I pass, that B grade from Santa Claus dramatically influenced my life's journey.

I completed my BS requirements in March 1964, as Penn State used the quarter system instead of semesters. My wife, Marjorie, had three months left on her teaching contract in Tyrone, Pennsylvania. I had applied to Penn State's Master of Science program, but I was rejected. Obviously, my grades weren't worthy of gaining admission to graduate school.

I wasn't too concerned as I had already decided to leave engineering and enter law school. I vaguely imagined a future in patent law. Because of my high score on the LSAT (Law School Admission Test), I was accepted into the University of Michigan law program starting the summer of 1964. I had applied to Michigan based on the fact that it was rated as one of the top five law schools in the nation at that time.

Since I found myself with a free quarter, I decided to take mechanical engineering classes at Penn State as an unclassified student. Why not get a few graduate courses on my transcript before law school? It seemed like a great idea. Penn State had a provision whereby any graduate could take some classes after graduation as a non-degree candidate.

I paid my tuition and did the paperwork, but I needed an advisor to sign for my course selections. I was sent to Dr. Donald Olson, Associate Head of the Mechanical Engineering Department. He was surprised because he had never had an unclassified student before. Olson asked me why I wasn't a Master's degree-seeking student. I explained that I had applied but had been denied admission.

He then asked me one question: "What grade did you get in DEQ?"

I replied, "B."

Dr. Olson told me to wait in his office. He left, then returned five minutes later with some papers in hand. He said, "If anybody wants to go to school that bad, we won't stop him."

I went home that night and told Marjorie that I was now admitted to Penn State as a degree program graduate student. Without a doubt, my B grade from Professor Rodgers in DEQ changed the entire direction of my life.

It's hard to second-guess all the what-ifs in life. Frankly, I can't even imagine what my life would have been like if I had gone on to law school.

I originally intended to remain at Penn State for just one additional year for my Master of Science degree and then go to law school at Michigan in 1965. That never happened because once I was in the master's program at Penn State I had better classes and better professors than I'd had in my undergraduate program. I liked control systems and eventually decided to go for my PhD in mechanical engineering with a major in control systems.

I find it ironic that as I built my professional career, I ultimately became an authority of sorts in DEQ. I say that because my entire professional life has been focused on unraveling various mysteries related to how things move, wiggle, and shake. Such movements are the essence of DEQ.

As I neared the end of my MS degree requirements, I applied to the Penn State PhD program and was again turned down. This is when Purdue University accepted me in 1965. Purdue was by far the best school in control systems of the five schools I had applied to. In fact, the only better school offering a doctorate in controls anywhere was MIT. Purdue University turned out to be the absolute best place for me. It served as the springboard to the future of my life and professional career.

Purdue and MIT had differing philosophies as to what constitutes control systems. MIT's program was based on ODEs structured with matrices and with a focus on linear quadratic optimal control. Purdue was structured on the very practical work of Dr. Rufus Oldenburger, with an emphasis on industrial applications. Rufus Oldenburger, with a PhD in mathematics, cut his teeth on industrial control systems when he headed research at Woodward Governor in the WWII era. My doctoral advisor at Purdue was Dr. R. E. "Gene" Goodson, who studied under Oldenburger.

At the risk of being too lengthy, I want to comment about my mother's perceptions of me, especially as related to my academic pursuits. My mother, Ellen Kristensen Klein (1914-2002), was born in Denmark. She came to America at the age of 12, arriving at Ellis Island on September 15, 1926.

My mother learned English as a formal set of rules. In contrast, I never learned English in any formal sense. I just lived it and spoke it. Mother told me my usage of English violated many rules. Spelling was another issue. She once complained when I spelled a word as "illude" in a letter to her, telling me that such a word doesn't exist. I might have meant "allude" or possibly "elude." I don't remember. To her dying day, she had difficulty accepting the fact that I had somehow become a professor.

It wasn't until about 2008 that a friend explained to me my method of English usage. The friend, Annie, taught English as a second language. It was Annie's assessment that my mother was a *prescriptive* speaker of English, whereas I was a *descriptive* speaker. The formal rules have never concerned me and, quite frankly, never will. I focus on using words as they flow from within me to describe my thoughts and ideas. This flow from within comes from the subconscious level.

My mother was filled with negative images and expectations of me. Near the end of her life, she even confided that she had pictured me landing in jail someday, certainly not becoming an esteemed educator. I never pushed the matter to inquire why she had come to that view. However, I can take comfort in knowing that at least she didn't single me out. She didn't expect much of my two older brothers, Donald and Frederick, either. My oldest brother, Donald (1935-2016), got his PhD from Penn State. He became a Professor of Microbiology and spent the bulk of his professional career teaching at Colorado State University in Fort Collins, Colorado. My brother Fred spent his life working for the Federal Aviation Administration in North Carolina. If an aircraft crashed and the news announcement stated, "The F.A.A. is investigating," that meant Fred was on the job. He once commented that a common characteristic of plane crashes is that, when in trouble, the pilot decided to keep secrets. Yet when you are in trouble, others can't help you if you maintain radio silence.

I wasn't a perfect child, but I didn't deserve the constant criticism my mother gave me. Despite that negative and unsupportive environment, I have hopefully contributed in making the world a better place. I have also made a personal resolution to always support my children, my grandchildren, and, by extension, many others. Following the lead of Professor Rodgers, throughout my teaching career I tended to be liberal in dispensing grades. I believe students learned more in my classes, and that justifies the higher grades I gave them.

1963. Marjorie Ann Maxwell of Walcott, Iowa, and I were joined in marriage. I started dating Marjorie while we were attending the University of Iowa. The marriage festivities took place at the First Presbyterian Church of Davenport.

Following the wedding, the Kleins took up residence in Tyrone, Pennsylvania, close to State College, Pennsylvania, so that I could complete my BS degree in mechanical engineering at Penn State. Marjorie taught kindergarten in various local schools, one year in Tyrone and one year in State College.

On November 22, 1963, President John F. Kennedy was assassinated while in a motorcade in Dallas, Texas. This event came as a great shock to our nation. Many who were alive then can describe where they were at the time and how the news affected them. It was mid-day, following my brown bag lunch break. I was walking into the Office of the Dean of Engineering, located on the first floor of the Hammond Building. I was planning to meet with Associate Dean Perez to request approval to take a Theoretical and Applied Mechanics course on vibrations in place of a somewhat similar course in mechanical engineering. I'd been hoping the switch would ease a scheduling conflict for the upcoming quarter. As I walked in, the entire office was silent. A group was huddled by a radio. I sensed that something was dreadfully wrong, but my instinct was to maintain my stride, hoping that the bad news would somehow vanish if I just kept on walking. It didn't.

1964. In my last year as an undergraduate at Penn State, I was introduced to the study of control systems through an elective course. Many texts on this topic are available for readers seeking an overview; one classic reference is the text by Benjamin Kuo [3]. Even at Penn State, the number of available elective courses was limited. I needed the credit so I took the dual senior/graduate level course. It was challenging. I did so poorly that I received a D grade. I ended up taking the course again as a graduate student for my masters. On the second go-round, I managed to get a B. Nonetheless, my fascination with systems theory became so strong that my MS Thesis [4] was on the topic of adaptive control.

The word *adaptive* is starkly distinct from the somewhat similar word *adapted*. When one speaks of adapted physical activity, for example, the word *adapted* implies that the activity has been changed so that persons with specified disabilities or limitations can better participate. In contrast, *adaptive* as used in systems theory terminology relates to an internal, thus self-organizing, logic structure within a system. The system itself adapts and changes, making it adaptive. The adaptive process works markedly better when the underlying process is stable.

As it relates to the process of learning how to ride a bike, the adaptive processing works best when the bike isn't continually falling over. When the bike is modified to not fall over, the struggling rider is better able to engage in the learning or adaptive process. The rider then adapts his or her feedback reactions and motor plans.

1965. I applied to Purdue University's doctoral program in mechanical engineering and was accepted. I had applied to five schools, including Penn State, and was rejected by four. However, I only needed one acceptance.

My Graduate Record Exam score of 87th percentile got me into Purdue. At that time Purdue used a minimum GRE score in Engineering of 75th percentile as its admission cut-off, placing lesser weight on past grades. Luckily for me, Purdue had been my first choice.

I had finished my MS work at Penn State in late summer of 1965. In September, Marjorie and I took up residence in an apartment in West Lafayette, Indiana. Marjorie took on a teaching job in the West Lafayette school system. We were close enough to our respective schools that she could walk to work and I could walk to school.

Although my GRE score got me admitted, I was initially denied financial aid. By the second semester at Purdue, I was offered an assistantship, which allowed me to become a member of the club—I was given an office cubicle and allowed fellowship with other graduate students. My other financial aid package was known as a "blonde" scholarship, as Marjorie's full time teaching salary is what we lived on.

1966. While I was at Purdue, I approached Dr. R. E. "Gene" Goodson to serve as my doctoral thesis advisor, and he accepted me. He soon after took a semester's leave of absence to work for Corning Glass Company in Corning, New York. As I was one of his students, he arranged a summer internship for me at Corning Glass working in conjunction with him.

I assisted Goodson with a computer simulation of massive proportions on a component in glass-making called the fore hearth. Think of it as a large oven (about 100 feet long) that channels molten glass as it cools sufficiently to then be drawn into desired glass products. The purpose of the fore hearth is to control the cooling of the molten glass as it comes out of the main oven. That computer model, based mathematically on finite differences, was written in FORTRAN. The program was massive, containing 200,000 to 300,000 lines of code and requiring running time that was measured in days. We could only do one computer run a week, which was over the weekend when the Corning Glass mainframe digital computer was less busy.

This opportunity to work with Goodson was a professional milestone. I became proficient in FORTRAN as well as in the use of finite differences modeling in real world heat transfer applications. The basic heat transfer model of the fore hearth was complex. It was a time-dependent model as well as being spatially dependent, in that it was in three dimensions. Heat transfer in molten glass is a combination of conduction, mass transport, and finally radiation. Because glass remains clear when molten, the radiation transfers involve volume-to-volume radiation as well as surface-to-surface radiation. The finite-difference equations were in three dimensions with time as the fourth dimension. The developed model was highly nonlinear as well. Goodson set it up to employ relaxation techniques to unravel the cross dependency between mass transport and the change in viscosity as a function of temperature. The approach was complex, even revolutionary.

I emerged at the end of that summer with considerable knowledge about modelling and computer simulations of processes involving highly complex heat and mass transport dynamics. Said in other terms, I knew then (and still know) more about heat balances and heat transfer than the vast majority of the world's present climate change pundits.

Two pleasurable aspects of that summer at Corning were water skiing on the Finger Lakes and having sufficient time to start taking private pilot flying lessons.

1968. During the decade that followed Sputnik (1958–1968), I was immersed in America's race to beat the Russians to the moon. Within the mechanical engineering faculty, Purdue had a dedicated control systems group led by Dr. Rufus Oldenburger, a giant in the field. I hoped to be hired into that group after graduation. But by then, Purdue had adopted a policy of not hiring their own graduates. Purdue already had too many of their graduates as faculty, so their goal was to terminate what was aptly described as academic inbreeding. I then set my sights on other schools.

On April 18, 1968, I passed my flight test. I was now a licensed private pilot. My reason for mentioning my pilot qualifications has to do with human operation of a vehicle that is subject to roll and yaw. Flying an airplane and riding a bike share certain commonalities. My flight training afforded me insights into the nuances of teaching children how to master bike riding.

The Rocket Scientist Perspective. I graduated from Purdue University with a PhD in control systems. Basically, I had become a full-fledged rocket scientist. If you want to be in the rocket business, you must do two things: propel the rocket and guide the rocket. Recall that the Third Reich's dangerous V-1 and V-2 rockets aimed at London during WWII were notoriously inaccurate. Hitler's rockets lacked proper guidance systems, so many of the V-1s and V-2s did little damage as they frequently missed their mark, hitting wooded areas around London's suburbs instead. I was in the guidance side of the rocket business.

As my studies at Purdue University drew to a close, I realized that going into industry was out of the question. Marjorie and I had our sights firmly set on academia. We have always enjoyed three aspects of teaching: June, July, and August. I interviewed with Tennessee Tech in Cookeville, Tennessee for a teaching position. Tennessee Tech had an undergraduate mechanical engineering degree program, but not a graduate program.

Through this experience, I realized I wanted something more encompassing, notably a school with a graduate program in mechanical engineering.

In my naïveté, I had somehow concluded that getting a shot at an academic position would be unlikely, or at least limited. I had images of filled slots and believed that an opening would only rarely occur, most likely due to the death or retirement of some aged professor. With that view in mind, I cast a wide net. I decided I didn't like living and commuting daily in a big city, defined as any city large enough to have a flying reporter giving radio coverage of rush hour traffic jams. The school had to have an accredited degree-granting mechanical engineering program, and it needed to be in a small town. Fifty schools nationwide met this requirement. Marjorie and I then sent out 50 letters, each with a résumé and a cover letter stating my interest in an academic position.

To my astonishment, within several days, the phone in our apartment in West Lafayette literally rang off the hook. As people called, they would introduce themselves by name, but I had lost track as to what school Dr. X was calling from. I soon realized I needed to keep a tablet of names and addresses next to the telephone.

One irony is that Michigan State had rejected me as a doctoral student in 1965. Yet just three years later with my PhD sheepskin in hand, Michigan State invited me to interview for a tenure-track faculty position. I turned them down.

One thing in my favor once I started sending out résumés rested in my area of expertise: control systems.

To put this into perspective, the national *Accreditation Board for Engineering and Technology* (ABET), quite unknown to me at the time, had recently mandated that all accredited undergraduate mechanical engineering degree-granting schools within the U.S. include a required undergraduate course in control systems. Schools nationwide went into a mad scramble to come up with qualified staff in that specific area. I became a highly sought-after addition to many schools. Job offers came in so fast that I could barely keep track of them. Bradley University in Peoria made me an offer over the telephone without even having interviewed me. Likewise, I received a telephone offer of a faculty position from the University of North Dakota in Fargo, bypassing the need for an on-site interview. The University of Wisconsin at Madison expressed interest in hiring me, but hadn't yet added a line item for my salary in their budget. It was their intention to hire me on what is called soft money, with the promise that a line item would be applied for. I thanked them and said no thank you. Roughly 20 schools invited me for recruiting visits. In the end, I visited seven schools and received employment offers from all seven.

My ability to rise from the ashes of my unexceptional childhood and lackluster high school years, much like the phoenix in Greek mythology, was nothing short of a miracle.

Sinking Roots at the University of Illinois (1968–1971)

IN SEPTEMBER 1968 I accepted a position as Assistant Professor at the University of Illinois in Urbana-Champaign. I selected Illinois for four reasons.

First, it was the most prestigious. My plan was to stay three to five years and then go to a smaller school to get a spot as a department head. I reasoned that for a position higher on the ladder, I would have to move to a lesser school. "It's a good place to leave," I rationalized to myself upon accepting the offer.

Second, the department head at Illinois, Dr. Helmet Korst, made a persuasive case that additional staff in my area would be hired and I would be given the leadership role of that group.

Third, Marjorie was offered substantially more money by the Champaign school district than most competing schools. She had received offers as a public school teacher from the same cities where I'd received offers, so we looked at the combined salaries. Her offers varied greatly. Schools in the south, including Gainesville, Florida, and Cookeville, Tennessee, offered only about half of what Champaign offered her.

A fourth reason was the proximity to family. Marjorie's family in Eastern Iowa was a short drive away.

My job at Illinois was to do research and teach mechanical engineering classes related to systems dynamics and control. As events unfolded, I remained at the University of Illinois for three decades, eventually retiring in 1998.

Settling into Urbana-Champaign, Illinois. In 1968, as Marjorie and I settled into Urbana-Champaign, the future seemed limitless. Marjorie and I lamented the absence of lakes and mountains, but even for that we had a plan. While in graduate school at Purdue, I had taken more flying lessons. And in April I had become a licensed private pilot. Our plan was to use a single-engine private airplane to make jaunts to prettier places. We even hoped to eventually buy a lake property in Wisconsin and fly there on weekends.

1969. The year 1969 brought an abrupt halt to the post-Sputnik era. Three circumstances contributed:
1. Americans landed on the moon and safely returned to Earth. Following a decade of hype, the moon walk itself was anti-climactic. A Peanuts cartoon featuring Snoopy summed it up. Snoopy said (paraphrased) as he lay dejected next to his doghouse, "If we can get to the moon, why then do I have to sleep in a doghouse?"
2. Vietnam War protests were tearing the country and higher education apart. Protesters at the University of Illinois targeted the Center for Advanced Computation that housed the Illiac IV—then one of the world's most powerful computers—because it had been funded with Department of Defense (DoD) money.
3. Racial unrest was rampant. In Champaign, the racial strife was so intense that police cars only rarely ventured into the city's "North End." Sgt. Bill Newman's squad car was hit

with 126 bullets merely by entering the hostile area of town in broad daylight. It was said at the time that Sgt. Newman survived as he had the sense to hide himself using the vehicle's engine block as a shield. Champaign's North End took on the character of a war zone. Marjorie taught kindergarten in the southwest (more affluent) area of Champaign. Some kids were bused into her school from the North End. She asked a boy why he was continually falling asleep in school. The answer was, "My Momma made me sleep in the bathtub." Bullets were flying randomly through the thin walls of the public housing projects. The kids were deemed to be safer if they were protected by the cast iron bathtub. Most shots being fired stemmed from turf battles between rival gangs engaged in shooting wars.

The end of the post-Sputnik era boded poorly for higher education funding. Technical education that could be deemed an extension of the despised "industrial-military complex" became the central target for funding cuts. At the University of Illinois, war protesters took over the Illini Student Union. They tore down the draperies and set them on fire in a heap inside the Union. That single incident destroyed $50,000 worth of draperies and caused substantial smoke damage to the building's interior. In response, the Illinois General Assembly slashed funding for higher education.

One year prior to my being hired, I was promised that four additional staff would be hired under me and that I would be the head of a controls group. I envisioned the new group to be on par with Purdue University.

"Victory has 100 fathers; defeat is but an orphan." That quote, paraphrased, has been attributed to the German Commander General von Rundstedt directly following the Allied landing of D-Day. In my case *circa* 1969, the funding tide had done a complete 180, but nobody had the fortitude to even inform me. I was left to figure out what had happened myself. The lavish promises from 1968 had vanished in a wink.

Along the way I made an error of sorts. I did my job too well. While similar mechanical engineering programs at other schools required multiple professors, I was able to handle it myself. I taught the required undergraduate control systems courses without needing the four additional staff Dr. Korst had promised me.

The Mechanical Engineering building on campus had mostly small classrooms, sized to handle about 25 to 30 students. When the building was originally built in the days between WWI and WWII, classes were small, often with students working on drafting tables. I was typically assigned the two larger lecture rooms, which could handle 60 students each, as I often had large class sizes. As I recall, Illinois was then graduating about 240 mechanical engineering undergraduates each year. Half of those students would take the controls class in the fall semester, and the other half would take it in the spring semester. For several years, it was normal for me to teach all four sections: two sections each semester with up to 60 students in each section.

One can handle large teaching loads for a while, but at some point exhaustion sets in. And each course generates what I call door traffic. Students seek out the professor for any number of reasons. I maintained an "open door policy" where students could stop by as long as my office door was open, which it usually was. (I will interject that I never closed the door if a student was in the office.) Students discovered that the best time to catch me was over lunch hour, since I always brown bagged my lunch.

I could handle the load. It was just a matter of maintaining my sanity. In the end, it was more than a decade before an extra staff member was hired.

As the post-Sputnik era's ending came, my department's budget was slashed. Hiring was frozen. My dream of heading the controls group was crushed—there was no group to head. Instead of building a foundation in my area, I was assigned to teach other subjects where there were staff shortages, including a heat transfer class and a particularly dreadful statistical thermodynamics course for electrical engineers who had scant interest in the topic. It was a dismal first year teaching at Illinois.

As an academic in a specific discipline, I was isolated without colleagues to collaborate with. Though the Electrical Engineering department at Illinois had a strong core of controls people, I was an outsider. Polite as they were, they had their critical mass and didn't need me. This isolation shaped, in part, my future research, which was to venture into areas where I didn't need colleagues, a research group behind me, or a research budget.

Over the years as Marjorie took more advanced coursework in education, I became aware of the writings of educator Dr. Benjamin S. Bloom. Professor "Bud" Konzo, associate head of the department at Illinois, also introduced me to Bloom's work. As a teacher, I was attracted to pedagogical approaches. Bloom served as editor to the book, *Taxonomy of Educational Objectives* [5]. In summary, Bloom's *Taxonomy* structured educational objectives as a six-level hierarchy:

1. **Knowledge** – Fact-level memorization of knowledge
2. **Understanding** – The facts
3. **Application** – The ability to use facts in a problem environment
4. **Analysis** – The ability to form central ideas
5. **Synthesis** – The ability to combine two ideas to create a new idea
6. **Evaluation** – The ability to examine a situation where some conflict in ideas exists and identify the underlying flaw

Whole books have been written on the topic, so please forgive my brief overview. For more information, I advise reading the many available books and papers on the topic.

Bloom's *Taxonomy*—and its implications for learning and creativity—became the bedrock I built my educational philosophy on. Most education focuses on the lower levels, whereas intellectual productivity in the workplace depends upon skills at the higher levels. I developed considerable disdain for the memorizer, and encouraged students to become proficient at the upper levels.

One of the things that later attracted me to the study of the bicycle was the conflict that existed in the literature concerning how and why bikes work. I found approximately 20 peer-reviewed scholarly papers on the bicycle, all of which disagreed with each other. I concluded that all 20 were flawed to varying degrees. Some experts, such as Dr. Andy Ruina of Cornell University, would disagree, saying that three papers out of the 20 were correct. My definition of a correct paper is more stringent. Because I invoke principles from control systems theory, I require a set of equations (pertaining to the bicycle model equations) to pass the *physical realizability* test. A discussion of physical realizability would entail arguments rooted in the calculus and is thus better left to academics. In the interest of brevity, I will not elaborate. Regarding an overview of the bicycle modeling papers, I am compelled to give a credit at this point: The MS Thesis by R. S. Hand [6] looked at 20 bicycle and motorcycle papers pertaining to answering the question of why a bike or motorcycle stays upright.

The upshot of this discussion is that considerable confusion abounded, even in scholarly literature, concerning why a bike can be ridden—and with such seeming ease.

1970. David Jones published an article called "The Stability of the Bicycle" on April 1, 1970, in *Physics Today* [7]. The article centered on his attempts to construct a bicycle that would be unrideable. Some speculated that the article was an April Fool's joke, but it wasn't. The article lingered in the back of my mind as bicycles and rockets share similarities in that they both need to be propelled, guided, and stabilized.

I spent the summer of 1970 as a resident consultant to Caterpillar Tractor Company in Peoria, Illinois. My assignment entailed studying a heavy articulated earth-moving vehicle. The sketch below provides the basic configuration. Considerable detail has been omitted as Caterpillar doesn't give its designs away for free. The purpose of the hinged joint in the center was to allow steering without need for Ackermann steering (having front wheels that turn). Instead, the entire front assembly can be turned. This permitted the engineering team at Caterpillar Tractor Company to arrive at a more durable and robust vehicle. The front wheels were powered, so this was an all-wheel-drive vehicle.

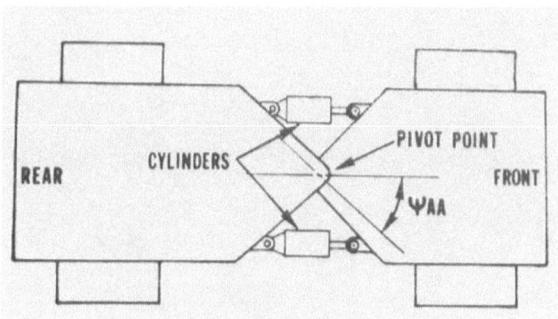

The fact that the articulated vehicle had a hinged center joint required a new look at the dynamics of objects that move but are subject to the presence of hinged joints, called kinematic constraints.

Bear in mind that a bicycle shares this same property. Bicycles are complex owing to the nature of the joints present. The frame tilts on the contact points. The front fork assembly is hinged to the frame by the steering tube and headset bearings. And riders can articulate or shift their upper torso as their body is seated on the saddle.

Caterpillar Tractor Company sought a U.S. Patent [8] on the steering system innovations. I am named as one of the four inventors on the patent.

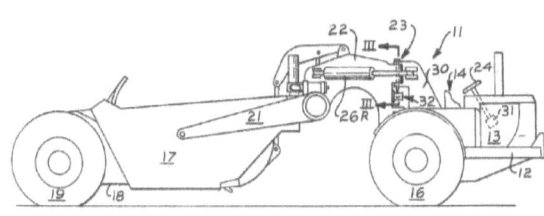

United States Patent [19]

Scholl et al.

[11] **3,795,285**

[45] **Mar. 5, 1974**

[54] STEERING SYSTEM FOR ARTICULATE VEHICLES

[75] Inventors: Rolland D. Scholl, Peoria; Edward J. Moyer, Morton; Terry W. Glynn, East Peoria; Richard E. Klein, Champaign, all of Ill.

[73] Assignee: Caterpillar Tractor Co., Peoria, Ill.

[22] Filed: **Apr. 3, 1972**

[21] Appl. No.: 240,588

[52] U.S. Cl. .... 180/79.2 B, 180/103, 307/66, 318/621

[51] Int. Cl. B62d 5/04, B62d 5/06

[58] Field of Search .... 180/79.1, 79.2 R, 79.2 B, 180/82 R, 103; 114/144 R; 307/48, 66; 318/587, 621, 663, 674; 340/249

[56] **References Cited**
UNITED STATES PATENTS

3,455,408	7/1969	Larsen	180/79.2 B
3,007,655	11/1961	Criswell et al.	180/79.1 X
3,465,276	9/1969	Silva et al.	318/621 X
3,440,435	4/1969	Sanders	307/66
3,387,684	6/1968	Belke et al.	180/79.1 X
3,662,243	5/1972	Cavil et al.	318/674 X
2,496,391	2/1950	Hall	318/621 X
2,729,750	1/1956	Draper et al.	307/66 X
3,577,003	5/1971	Behr et al.	307/66

Primary Examiner—Kenneth H. Betts
Assistant Examiner—Leslie J. Paperner
Attorney, Agent, or Firm—Fryer, Tjensvold, Phillips & Lempio

[57] **ABSTRACT**

The front frame of an articulated vehicle is pivoted relative to the back frame for steering purposes by fluid motors controlled through an electrically operated valve. The valve is controlled by the output of an amplifier which produces a signal indicative of the difference between a command signal obtained from a potentiometer coupled to the operator's steering wheel and an actual articulation signal from another potentiometer responsive to changes in the angle of the vehicle frames. Thus a difference between the position of the steering wheel and the actual articulation of the vehicle results in operations of the fluid motors to eliminate such difference. A phase lag is provided in the feedback loop defined by the system to counteract the effects of oil mass resonance which otherwise causes instability unless steps are taken that have adverse side effects such as slowing response and decreasing precision in fluid motor operated systems. Safety means are provided for maintaining electrical energization in the event of failure of the primary power supply and for blocking starting of the vehicle engine if steering wheel position does not conform with actual articulation.

7 Claims, 8 Drawing Figures

1971. From a research standpoint, the first several years of my professorship at the University of Illinois were exciting and productive. I was being paid and accorded respect to do what I liked best: to think and to explore the world of ideas.

I made thrusts into several research areas, including:

1. Innovations in the stabilization of tall engineering structures, notably tall buildings subject to wind or earthquake excitations.

2. A climate hypothesis regarding the causation of glacial ages, and the dynamics related to the stability of the Earth's temperature balance.

3. My findings in both areas were groundbreaking (in my view), but getting entrenched experts to accept my seemingly radical ideas was an entirely different matter.

Because of the frustrations I encountered in those areas, I eventually set them aside and cast my sights onto new areas to explore. The one that took center-stage was bicycle research.

My Professorship: The Mid-Years (1972-1981)

BY THE LATE 1970S, after leaving behind the frustrations of research in structural control and glacial causation, I decided to explore other areas of research. I sought topics where confusion abounded, where there was little competition, and where I had a means to prove my findings. Validating findings related to bicycles would be vastly easier than structures or climate.

As a young assistant professor in the early 1970s, I understood that one obligation was to procure outside funding. I prepared a grant proposal for submission to the National Science Foundation (NSF). The proposed research involved tall structures and was for about $110,000 annually, for a total of three years. After including the usual overhead charge imposed by the University of Illinois, the grant request total came to about $500,000. Before being mailed out, the proposal required the signature of the Head of the Department.

I made an appointment with Dr. Helmet Korst. Dr. Korst, an Austrian, was a world-renowned expert in gas dynamics. He and I got along well, as we respected each other's expertise in mathematics and abstract thinking. Recall that it was Dr. Korst who made the offer for me to come to Illinois.

To better understand the backdrop to the situation, I need to provide some context. At the time, the departmental faculty numbered about 50 professors, most hired in the 1940s to handle the post-war influx of G.I.s coming back from the war and going to school. The mechanical engineering department had hired 1930s-era graduates who were seeking advanced degrees, and let them teach undergraduate classes. These "teachers" tended to have master degrees or earned their MS degree while teaching, but in virtually all cases they did not have PhDs. Moreover, they functioned as teachers rather than researchers. Over half of the faculty were teachers only and didn't do research or write publications. When I entered in 1968 as an assistant professor with a PhD, I was a rarity.

For historical reasons I won't go into, the Mechanical Engineering Department at Illinois was a traditional teaching school, with drafting tables and a laboratory where steam engines were center stage. Digital computers and miniature calculators hadn't yet come into any significant usage. Engineering students carried slide rules that dangled from a belt loop in a leather case or scabbard, akin to swords. The building adjacent to the Mechanical Engineering Laboratory was the Foundry. Students learned foundry skills such as making sand molds and casting molten metal into desired shapes. All of that was to change.

Also at that time, a new Dean of Engineering, Dr. Daniel C. Drucker from Brown University, was demanding evidence of scholarly activities—meaning papers published in scholarly journals. Korst only had about five senior faculty conducting research and publishing; the bulk of the faculty produced zero scholarly papers. It's interesting to note that all of these senior faculty members had immigrated to the U.S. following WWII. American researchers with PhDs did exist, but they didn't populate the Mechanical Engineering Department at Illinois. Dr. Korst was under incredible pressure to demonstrate to the Dean of

Engineering that his department could produce papers. To quote Dean Drucker, "Zero is not arguable."

This is where I came into the picture. As a young theoretician, I could grab onto problems of all sorts and get papers published. My weapon was my specialization in the mathematical foundations of control systems theoretic principles, affording me numerous opportunities to enter into muddy areas and get publishable results. For one period, I was putting out more papers than the entire faculty combined. Dr. Korst wanted me to continue publishing papers and knew that redirecting my activities to funded research would only inhibit my ability to publish.

In my brief discussion with Dr. Korst, he glanced at my NSF draft proposal, folded it in half, and handed it back to me unsigned. Dr. Korst was a man of few words. He only said, "Dick, don't do this sort of thing."

I completely understood what Dr. Korst was saying. I was (and am) a theoretical thinker. For me to be productive as a faculty member, I needed only time to think, a desk, and possibly paper to write on. Dr. Korst fully recognized that my greatest contribution would come from my ideas, my creative thought processes. That flow of ideas would only be hampered by the drudgery of complying with writing periodic reports for NSF and other granting agencies—reports that nobody of any consequence would ever read. Dr. Korst said all this to me in his brief but sincere utterance.

That sentence wasn't in writing, but rather spoken from the depths of Dr. Korst's heart. I took his admonition seriously and stayed the course, following his wise counsel throughout my three decades at Illinois.

The problem was that times and power structures changed along the way. Several department heads later I had become an outcast in the department. Perhaps "leper" would be more appropriate. Meanwhile, most of the older faculty with only MS degrees faded away into retirement and/or slide rule heaven. In their places came sharp new PhD types who aggressively pursued outside funding. By the mid-to-late 1980s, generating outside funding had become the one and only measure of success and stature among faculty. The average funding generated per faculty member was several hundred thousand dollars annually. I brought in zero outside dollars. Politics and greed had transformed the university setting.

Dr. Korst had moved on and was no longer head. I had no interaction with the new department head. In fact, although my office was on the third floor of the Mechanical Engineering Building, I made a point of never taking the elevator. Elevators can trap you into exchanging niceties. Instead, I used the stairs and took the steps two at a time. If I encountered anybody, I kept moving so fast that only the briefest hello could transpire. It was also a great way to stay in shape.

In 10 years, I never exchanged one word with my department head beyond a quick hello. Nonetheless, I resolved to be true to what I did best—be a theoretical and even visionary thinker. I felt a sense of betrayal that I had done what the previous department head had directed and yet was now judged to be deficient because I had not brought money into the university's coffers.

The Schwinn Bicycle Company funded a research activity by R. Douglas Roland of the Cornell Aeronautical Laboratory concerning the bicycle. Roland published a paper [9] that gave the equations of motion for the bicycle with rider, and accompanied the equations with digital computer simulation findings. Roland did not publish his FORTRAN source code. Consequently, other researchers had no means of validating his findings. At the time, one of my colleagues argued that the mere existence of Rowland's findings made all other bicycle research pointless.

I took an entirely different view. The fact that a set of equations could replicate in a simulation the motion of a bicycle proved nothing other than to confirm that bicycles obey Newton's basic laws. By then digital computers had the ability to number crunch. What Rowland's work lacked was the ability to systematically perform synthesis to design a better bicycle, for example, one with improved behavioral characteristics.

In the back of my cynical mind, I viewed Schwinn's funding of such bicycle research as insurance to allow the company to better defend itself in future product liability lawsuits that might arise. Obviously bicyclists do get injured, and legions of attorneys are looking for the opportunity to sue somebody with deep pockets.

In 1975, although I had already been a licensed pilot for seven years, accumulating considerable hours of VFR (Visual Flight Rules) flight time, I took and passed the check-ride to become an instrument rated (IFR, Instrument Flight Rules) pilot. Flying and bicycle riding have much in common. My pilot training, especially instrument flying, made my feedback senses more acute. Maintaining a proper scan rate is paramount, both in bike riding and flying.

My pilot experience also gave me insight into bicycle dynamics and stability, which came into play later when I began designing adaptive trainer bikes.

The Gradual Shift to Bicycles (1982–1986)

1982. I spent the summer of 1982 as a senior scientist at Hughes Aircraft Company, Missile Systems Division, in Canoga Park, California. My work involved mathematical modeling of the Phoenix-C, then a state-of-the-art and mainstay air-to-air missile in America's Cold War defense system. I was offered this opportunity by a former classmate from Purdue, Dr. William T. Carpenter (1943-2015). Bill served as head of Hughes Aircraft Company's missile systems guidance group, having been hired after finishing his doctorate at Purdue.

The photograph below shows Phoenix-C missiles under the wings and fuselage of the Navy's carrier-based F-14 Tomcat fighter aircraft. Each Tomcat carried a cluster of six missiles. Each air-to-air missile was approximately 15 inches in diameter, 13 feet in length, and weighed 1,030 pounds. Upon activation, the Phoenix-C was deployed from the mother aircraft using explosive bolts. The abrupt ejection would at times cause unwanted axial bending. My objective in modeling the missile was to allow the Hughes Aircraft engineers to better understand the bending modes.

Like the Caterpillar heavy truck and the bicycle, the Phoenix-C missile shared the attributes of hinged joints. This occurred because of the flexible nature of the missile combined with the presence of the hinged control surfaces (fins for steering and guidance).

My experience at Hughes Aircraft was eye-opening. The engineers used this incredible FORTRAN subroutine to easily unravel and otherwise clean up the mathematical mess caused by the hinged joints. Yet even though the United States' defenses during the Cold War era relied considerably on the Phoenix-C, which was designed using this subroutine, these engineers had no clue as to the mathematics that made the subroutine work.

I obtained permission to take a copy of the subroutine back to Illinois at the end of the summer. Hughes had no concerns about security breaches. The real secrets in the missile business were the actual hardware and the missile's performance specifications. The theory that made the missiles work wasn't considered a security concern.

In the fall semester of 1982 I had a class of about 60 students. Just as students can experience a bad semester, it turned out to be a difficult semester for me. Teaching was harder than usual; the students did not do as well. My fault? Their fault? In the end, blame needn't be assigned. One just moves on and tries to do better.

Consequently, I gave out somewhat lower grades that semester compared to my norm. A group of about six to eight students came to my office to ask if I would consider raising their grades. I explained that I was a reasonable person. I would need some form of evidence of their knowledge of the material. In my view, I was teaching material akin to a foreign language. The real test would be their ability to apply that language to a topic.

My challenge to them was to go home for the usual end-of-semester break and upon returning submit to me a written essay in engineering language as to how and why a bike works. The bicycle is a dynamic system. It is subject to inputs, disturbances, and stability issues. Differential equations dictated the dynamics.

I also laid out ground rules. As a take-home assignment, obviously some would seek assistance from more knowledgeable people. My instructions were to use whatever resources they wished, or even could afford, but that they must understand their essay and be able to defend it orally.

Most of the essays were relatively dismal, but I was astonished with one student's essay. The student's name was Mary, and her essay was meticulous in detail. It was obvious that an experienced engineer had written it. Under my rules, that was perfectly acceptable as long as Mary could orally defend it.

I asked Mary who wrote the essay. She answered that her father did. I inquired further. The father was an engineering manager in a company in New Jersey. He had spent a week researching and writing the essay. Recall that in 1982, things we take for granted now like the internet and email were far from commonplace. Mary's father had dictated the essay to her word by word over the phone. Interestingly, although the essay was exceptional, the opening sentence was incorrect. The assertion was that the bicycle would fall over if there was no rider control. Evidence had shown me that a bike or motorcycle with ample speed is capable of remaining upright on its own.

It was at this point that I discovered the bicycle as a teaching tool. I decided to make this a required assignment for all my students in future semesters. Because I was teaching large classes at the University of Illinois and because of my faith in the Socratic method of teaching, I challenged the students to write about how and why a bike works. This activity started in earnest in the spring of '83.

Incidentally, I did raise the grades of most of the students who came to me in December. In Mary's case, her grade went from "C" to "A." She was able to orally defend the essay since her father had instructed her well. Mary will reappear some 22 years later, so stay tuned.

1983. Many Americans were glued to the television screen as the farewell to $M^*A^*S^*H$ aired in a two-hour special. Captain Benjamin "Hawkeye" Pierce had feigned insanity for years, but in the final episode Hawkeye went over the brink.

As a side note illustrating the extent of the popularity of the show's finale, the chart below recorded the city's water pressure in Champaign, Illinois, on the night of the $M^*A^*S^*H$ finale. The pressure fluctuations, notably the pressure drop at the program's end at 10 p.m. local time, was the most severe pressure drop experienced by Northern Illinois Water Company in its history up to that date. This was due to everyone flushing the toilet at the same time—after two hours of rapt attention, not wanting to leave their seats, everyone finally had a chance to go. About 106 million people watched the finale, setting a record that has never been broken. In New York City alone, one million people used the toilet after the show—amounting to 15% of city's population flushing at once [10].

The water pressure record below was provided to me by a student at the time whose father was the President of Northern Illinois Water Company. The student was aware of my interest in $M^*A^*S^*H$ and its storylines.

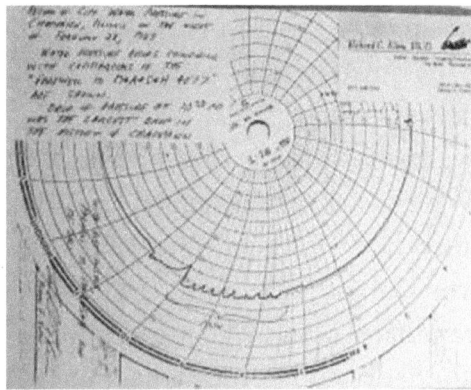

Similar to the $M^*A^*S^*H$ madness experienced by the battlefield surgeon, my teaching load at the University of Illinois had begun to overwhelm me. Much like Hawkeye, after thousands of students and countless lectures, I adopted a survival mode wherein I did what some might describe as insanity. I demanded that my students explain to me, in writing and for a grade, how and why a bike works. Bear in mind that this topic isn't addressed in the regular textbooks.

The pedagogical approach I adopted is referred to in educational terminology as *shared inquiry*. I asked questions of my students to which even I did not know the answers. This went on for about eight years. In that time, I had approximately 800 engineering students write essays on varied questions related to bicycle dynamics and stability.

After the first year, I changed the assignment to delve into specific aspects of bicycle stability and dynamics. For example, some semesters focused on topics such as:

- What role does gyroscopic action (precession) play in bike handling?
- What role does the geometry (shape) of the front fork play?
- Is it possible to ride a bike in a partial gravity environment, such as on the moon?
- Can one ride a bike that is rear steered?

- What is involved in riding a bike with no hands?
- What parameters will allow us to alter the critical velocity of a bike?
- Can we build a robotic bike—a bike with no rider?
- Are all bikes counter-intuitive, or can we design a bike that steers like a four-wheeled vehicle?
- And very importantly, how could we design a bike for children that would make it easier to learn how to ride?

Based on both theory and experiment, I knew that the stability of the bicycle is strongly influenced by proper fore-to-aft placement of the center of mass. Therefore, banana seats are not good for the learning rider because the rider's mass is too far back. I asked students to investigate fore-to-aft mass placement and the resulting effect as it related to stability, handling, etc.

The students typically worked in groups of three or four. Some of the essays were based on physical experiments where the students had altered the bikes to investigate a stated hypothesis. In all, about 250 essays were turned in. Of those essays, half were doubtful, a quarter of them were sort of okay, and a quarter were outstanding. By the late 1980s, I had accumulated around 60 top-rank research papers related to the bicycle and its stability. I was sitting on more bicycle research than any other person in the world. To this day, I still have copies of all those essays.

I've been asked why I didn't make those findings available to other researchers. The main reason is that I would not and could not publish the work of my students without their permission. Another reason is that an essay might have stated claims, but I lacked absolute verification of the conclusions. In order to publish, I would be required to replicate the experiments and findings, a daunting task.

In 2005 I did co-author with two Swedish colleagues a paper subsequently published in the *IEEE Control Systems Magazine* [11]. This paper reported on the best of the student findings, the cream of the crop. That paper received significant recognition and was later honored by IEEE as being the best paper out of several thousand published by IEEE that year.

1985. After several years, my bicycle essay assignment caused some discomfort among students. One student explained his dilemma. He intended to go on to medical school after engineering. He had to have an A in my course, but the essay assignment couldn't be resolved by simply memorizing facts and repeating them back on an exam. Much of the existing literature on the topic was wrong, and students who merely repeated some published statement often became victims of my red pen. He complained that even the past essays (which I made available in the university library) were no help because I'd marked much of their work as wrong too.

I proposed a solution to address the student's predicament: saw a bicycle in half and devise an experiment after rebuilding it in a different configuration. Push the bike down a hill and report the outcome. Reality does not lie! Write the essay based on the outcome of an experiment, and you can never be wrong.

And so it happened that my students relied less on theory and more on experiments. Instead of adding to confusion, my students and I collectively started to come up with solid answers. This is what kicked the bike program into high gear. Given dozens upon dozens of experimental outcomes, the nebulous mystery of the bike came into clear view.

1986. When validating what initially starts as theoretical insight, often the best proof of any candidate concept is an implementation of the concept in the real thing. Let's contrast three areas of research: control of tall buildings based on active feedback principles, glacial causation, and bicycle dynamics.

Compared to the first two research areas, the bicycle is a lone researcher's paradise. Bikes are plentiful. I could acquire bikes easily and for a modest budget. At a police auction I once purchased about 80 bicycles for under $100 total. I had access to the necessary machine shop tools to manufacture a prototype as might be required. The time scale associated with a bicycle-related experiment is short compared to the human lifespan. I didn't require the approval of a building owner or city regulator. I didn't have to fight with politicians who have claimed the public policy related to climate change as their exclusive turf. Few people, including colleagues, had life-or-death opinions about bicycles. Quite frankly, my dabbling into bicycle research was considered harmless and even ignored or ridiculed by many.

I induced my many students to take on the role of colleagues. Yes, some students objected, but I had what I wanted: sufficient numbers of capable and talented students who grabbed on to the idea of performing fun and yet groundbreaking research.

To add to all this, the bicycle literature was in chaos at that time, as some papers existed but many had come to differing and even opposing conclusions. We had our work cut out for us.

One aspect of the bicycle project focused on how children learn. Some students and I started working with a handful of children around seven years of age. We were able to find plenty of parents who would schedule an appointment with us, and during our session we would repeatedly launch their child on a bike. In the process of working with these children, my engineering students ended up doing a lot of running. We worked in the fall semester of 1986 with 10 children in all. Our observations were unexpected and even shocking. Nine of the 10 children went through four distinct phases, and they each required approximately 44 minutes to master bike riding.

The remaining child, the tenth, also mastered bike riding but didn't progress through the four phases. In this case, the boy's father was present, shouting out commands and orders. My assumption at the time was that the child simply froze on the bike and did not attempt to steer. His arms remained locked at the elbows. After all, when one is subjected to a constant barrage of criticism, a plausible motor plan is to freeze and do nothing. But much to our astonishment, as we approached the 44-minute mark, this last child went from doing nothing to virtual mastery of the bike: steering, pedaling, and coming to a stop.

We started the clock for each child at the first launch and ran the clock ran continuously, including time spent walking back up the street's incline.

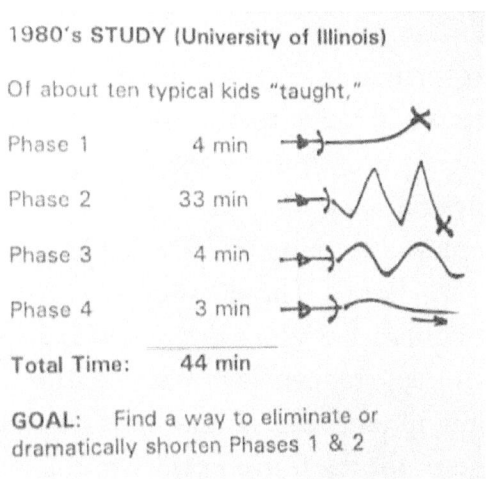

1980's STUDY (University of Illinois)

Of about ten typical kids "taught,"

Phase 1	4 min	
Phase 2	33 min	
Phase 3	4 min	
Phase 4	3 min	
Total Time:	**44 min**	

GOAL: Find a way to eliminate or dramatically shorten Phases 1 & 2

In the first two phases, which consumed 37 minutes, the bike oscillated and then fell over. It became obvious to me that we needed to modify the bike, just as modern aircraft can be modified, by what is called compensation. The goal became to modify the bike and consequently the environment experienced by the child.

Our next step was to create a trainer bike with more benign dynamics. The trainer would function as a *stable attractor*, to borrow terminology from chaos and fractal theory. Once stability can be assured—the bike isn't continually falling over—the child can adapt and learn quickly. That sums up the process of learning to ride a bike.

Contrary to most physical tasks that have to be learned and mastered, the human's ability to ride a bicycle comes as a sudden and adaptive realization. The inclusion of the word *adaptive* implies that the child is undergoing a transformation. The child is improving and refining his or her motor plan and motor planning.

The "aha" moment triggers one key counterintuitive ingredient—to turn the handlebars into the direction of the bicycle's fall. This happens in a brief moment of realization and is totally opposite to the intuitive prior reaction of resisting the fall, thus turning away from the fall.

Activities such as jumping rope, swimming, catching a ball, throwing a ball, and striking a pitched baseball with a bat are honed far more gradually. Yes, exceptional people can do things right away, and we describe these people as "naturals." Excluding the born naturals, most humans need considerable practice to master most physical skills.

In stark contrast, learning to ride a bicycle happens over a vastly shorter time frame. The question of whether a person can ride a bike has a binary answer: either yes or no. Once balancing is achieved, all other refinements like starting, braking, and navigation follow in rapid succession—often within a few minutes. It is only necessary for the learning rider to maintain speed and to nudge the steering into the direction of fall.

Unfortunately, numerous well-meaning but misinformed spotters are misguided about what is going on. Far too many spotters insist on holding onto the bike. Yes, the bike and rider wobble in the first moments following the initial launch. But when the spotter intervenes, it diminishes the rider's ability to refine their balancing skills. When spotting behind the learning child, the spotter must refrain from grasping onto the bike or training handle, if so equipped. The seeming initial erratic zig-zag pattern of the birthing rider is to be expected. The zig-zag stems from the time required for mental processing. If the spotter can just let go, the rider's zig-zagging will usually extinguish itself in a few minutes without any intervention from the spotter. After all, it's common knowledge that riding a bike is "as easy as riding a bike." Far too many people make far too much of something that is inherently so simple and natural.

The fundamentals of proper spotting are elaborated on in my book *Bikes Are Big on Planet Klynia* [12].

The work my students and I were doing with children led us to one primary task: making a trainer bike that stabilized the learning rider. For heavy Caterpillar trucks as well as fighter aircraft and missiles, the dynamics—including stability—can be tailored using compensation. This is often accomplished by the incorporation of circuitry within the control systems dynamic loop. For aircraft, the net result is commonly dubbed as "fly-by-wire."

In 1986 I started my quest to design and build a trainer, a bike with modified (more gentle and benign) dynamics. Instead of electronics, I opted to use mechanical compensation. I didn't feel that the world was ready for a high-tech electronically controlled and stabilized bike.

The Focus on Bicycles Continues (1987–1995)

1987. By this time, I knew a lot about why a bike behaves as it does. As I continued my quest to build an adaptive training bike (or "trainer"), I kept these concepts in mind:

- Bikes need *critical velocity* to remain upright without rider intervention. Some of the bike's physical parameters can be adjusted to raise or lower the critical velocity. For example, when the mass of the front wheel is increased, the bike's critical velocity is lower.

- The "aha" task of learning to ride a bike can be made easier with a properly designed trainer.

- Training wheels are largely counterproductive. They encourage an improper motor plan development—the child tends to shift their upper torso from side-to-side to achieve balance rather than learning to use handlebar steering corrections.

- The bike, when steered properly into the fall direction, involves counterintuitive tendencies. This explains what motorcyclists refer to as *counter-steering*.

- For the learning child, gravity acts as both enemy and friend. It needs to be tamed but not extinguished. Gravity can be countered by several means. I opted to use wide tires with a sufficiently generous lateral contour radius (LCR). I could somewhat tailor the LCR by changing the tire's inflation pressure.

- From my Master of Science thesis research on adaptive control, I knew that the bike should not be falling over. Learning best occurs when the system is stable versus constantly crashing.

- A child's learning process is typically a sudden and even cataclysmic event. Once the child discovers how the bike can be stabilized by suitable steering actions, the child's motor plan will adapt and fine-tune itself quickly, usually in a few minutes or less. The purpose of the trainer, with its subdued dynamics, was to trigger the "aha" moment.

Gravity was the one thing that drove the timescale, which dictated the speed of the action. Fearful children had difficulty learning to ride because the action was too fast. I had to slow down the action, specifically the rate of fall.

One solution would be to transport the children to another planet or to our moon, a body with a lower gravitational constant. NASA wasn't interested. A second option was to have the kids ride bikes underwater so that the water would support the body's mass. I also ruled that option out.

The third option was to mitigate gravity itself. I could see two obvious choices. The first was to use a wide tire similar in lateral profile to a rocking chair, allowing the bike to rock slightly side-to-side. Note that rocking chairs not only rock, they simultaneously lift the occupant. This is why rocking chairs typically don't fall over. The second way to mitigate gravity was to install compliant outriggers or spring-loaded training wheels. I chose a wide tire, which was ultimately replaced in later designs by a hard, contoured roller.

Under my direction, several students constructed the first trainer. This bike used turf tires, like you would find on powered lawn mowers and garden tractors. Starting in 1987 I used that turf-tired trainer to work with children. The results were outstanding.

The benefits of using wide tires, and later rollers, were obvious. I didn't have the slightest doubt as to the outcome. For readers interested in the theoretical benefits of a trainer bike utilizing wide tires, please refer to Appendix B for details of the physics behind it.

1988. A seemingly inconsequential event took place in 1988. Although obscure at the time, this near non-event played an important role in future happenings.

Students in my department at the University of Illinois participated in annual American Society of Mechanical Engineering (ASME) speaking contests and competed against teams from other schools at regional gatherings. I served as the ASME student chapter's faculty advisor and traveled with several students to a gathering in Louisville, Kentucky. We drove a departmental passenger van and took with us some research bikes to display and speak on, but not the turf-trainer.

A photographer from ASME took a picture of one bike that we claimed had zero-gyroscopic properties. It looked cool, and it got people's attention as well as sparking conversation. The bike shown below is one of my own photographs, not the photograph published by ASME.

A photograph similar to mine, but with a rider, subsequently appeared in the *ASME NEWS* newsletter [13]. A brief caption appeared with the photograph. No story, not even as much as a paragraph, just a caption stating that the bike had anti-gyroscopic properties and was a result of research at the University of Illinois. Beyond that, the photograph spoke for itself. The caption did not cite my name. That one photograph later, indeed years later, proved to be pivotal to the growth of the adaptive bike program.

The above photograph shows one of my students, Jadon Evans, riding the zero-gyroscopic bike. The correct word to use is *precession*, but for most people the word "precession" doesn't mean anything. Precession is a word from physics that denotes a reaction based on the conservation of angular momentum. The word "gyroscopic" brings to mind the image of a gyroscope. Because of this, I say things like zero-gyroscopic bike, but the correct terminology should instead be a zero-precession bike.

The bike was not only rideable; it was, in fact, easily rideable. The two upper wheels rested on the two lower wheels and counter-rotated, which cancelled the precession effects.

This bike created such a stir because many well-informed people bought into the assertion often made by physics instructors: the spinning action of the wheel is what makes it possible to ride a bike. The important word in that assertion is "is." As various experiments attested, gyroscopic action (precession) is helpful in bike riding, but it isn't the one and only thing that allows a bike to be ridden. That *necessity* assertion was proved to be patently false. The physics instructors making such claims had previously jumped to a conclusion but never tested the hypothesis with an actual bicycle experiment.

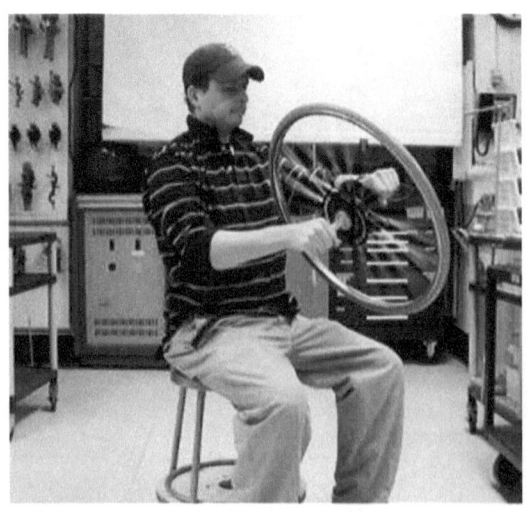

As shown above, we see the classic demonstration of someone sitting on a stool while holding a spinning bicycle wheel. Spinning the wheel and being twisted about when the axle is inclined isn't the same as actually riding a bike.

What usually occurs during the above demonstration is that the physics instructor or some know-it-all adds the remark, "And this is why a bicycle works." My numerous experiments with real precession-canceling bikes smashed that assertion to pieces. Once my students and I performed such experiments on real bikes, all arguments were terminated.

One of my favorite expressions is, "Reality doesn't lie." Conduct an experiment and the outcome will always reveal the truth. In keeping with the spirit of empiricism, which is rooted in experimentation, my students created and tested an array of experimental bicycles. Each experiment and its associated bike was constructed to solve a specific bicycle-related mystery. The results were outstanding, to say the least. A number of experimental bikes focused on issues related to precession and the role of precession in bike riding.

As an example, the bicycle shown above was configured to

find out if a person could ride a zero-precession bike without hands. The student, Dave Nagreski, is shown riding the bike with ease while using his hands. However, our attempts to ride "no handed" were unsuccessful. In any event, I can assure my readers that whenever we took our bikes out for public demonstrations, they were always crowd-pleasers.

In June 1988, I presented a paper [14] at the American Automatic Control Conference (AACC) in Atlanta, Georgia. The topic was on my teaching approach to systems theory with bicycles. The paper won an award for best paper of the session. The paper later appeared [15] in the April 1989 issue of the *Control Systems Magazine* published by IEEE.

The photograph below shows me along with many of the University of Illinois research bikes—and this collection contains just some of the bikes built by my students. The date of the photograph is *circa* 1988-1989.

1990. I tend to work slowly but steadily. Eight years after learning of the FORTRAN subroutine that unraveled the missile dynamics at Hughes Aircraft, I finally cracked the logic of the subroutine with the help of students. I proved why it worked as a stated theorem in mathematics.

I also concluded that the subroutine emanated from the research of Walter R. Evans (1920-1999), a noteworthy giant in the development of automatic control systems. Evans worked as an aerospace engineer at North American Rockwell (later to become Rockwell International). My colleagues at Hughes Aircraft acknowledged that the subroutine had originated at North American Rockwell. Walter Evans is considered to be the founder of what is now commonly known as the *root locus method*. His initial paper on that topic dates back to 1948. I suggest that the interested reader refer to the classic text in control systems by Truxal [16] for an overview of Evans' root locus method. Evans also included a chapter in his book *Control Systems Dynamics* [17] devoted to the use of determinants and the connection to Cramer's rule.

I submitted a manuscript to *IEEE, Transactions on Engineering Education*, which was accepted and published [18]. I could show that Cramer's Rule yielded the desired proof. I authored that paper as a contribution to the teaching of automatic control; I felt it would have been improper to claim credit for a finding that belonged rightly to Evans. I suspected that Evans had not published his work in any detail since the Rockwell subroutine bordered on national security matters. Unfortunately—or fortunately—the world moves on, and few people have noticed or cared. Nonetheless, I was comfortable in knowing that I had a mathematical foundation resting on bedrock for cutting through the equations that dictate the motion of a bicycle. The theorem and its corresponding FORTRAN code were analogous to the Jedi's light saber: with one foundational subroutine, I could cut through a myriad of complex mathematical models like a hot knife cutting through butter.

At this time, I experienced some serious medical issues. During a routine examination, my doctor detected an endocrine imbalance based on very reliable blood tests. The doctor wrote a letter to me, dated February 1989, documenting the diagnosis but he absentmindedly set it aside. I never received the letter because he never mailed it. Instead, he signed it and tucked it back into my medical file, where it was discovered several years later. My medical issues were not addressed until I went to the emergency room on December 23, 1990, almost two years later, with chest pains and shortness of breath.

Turns out I had Gull's disease, commonly known as hypothyroidism, which the body can reverse and recover from given adequate treatment and time. My medical condition was so extreme due to being left untreated for so long that my new doctor used the expression "a constellation of symptoms." I recall being in the hospital bed when interns would gather around as my doctor explained the varied symptoms associated with advanced hypothyroidism. In today's world of modern medicine, advanced cases of Gull's disease are rare. The doctor used me as a case example to show the interns and residents.

Because of my medical issues, I was granted medical leave for the spring semester of 1991. In the fall of 1991, I returned to limited teaching duties. It took several additional years for my body to recover. These are what I call the lost years.

1991. As our technology entered the last decade of the 1900s, many advances were made. Electronics became vastly more miniaturized, reliable, and affordable. I purchased a Sony Handi-Cam 8 mm video camera and started to record much of my bike activities and instructional work with children. The impact on the development of the bike program was substantial. I now had documentation as well as the ability to review activities I had recorded.

In June 1991 I presented an overview of my bike research at the International Federation of Automatic Control (IFAC) Advances in Controls Education Symposium in Boston, Massachusetts. The paper [19] was well received. I also made contact with several noteworthy people, one being Dr. Karl Astrom of Lund, Sweden. Dr. Astrom and I later collaborated on an article that appeared in 2005 [11].

1992. In the fall of 1992 I received a telephone call from Grant Pedersen, now a legend in the world of bicycling. At that time, he was the head of Bridgestone Cycling in the U.S., a branch of Bridgestone Tire Company based in Japan. Pedersen had been instructed to contact me by his superior in Japan, who had somehow seen the photograph of the precession-cancelling bicycle published in *ASME NEWS* some four years earlier. The Japanese executive must have taken considerable effort to identify me as the source since my name was not mentioned when the 1988 photograph was published by ASME.

When Pedersen called, he did not particularly want to talk to me. He explained his uncomfortable predicament over the phone and surely expected me to just hang up. If I did, he could report back to his boss that he had tried and that I had refused to talk to him.

I didn't hang up. After some time on the phone, I arranged to meet Pedersen at a bicycle trade show in northern Illinois. I brought along some of the University of Illinois experimental bikes. Upon seeing the bikes, Pedersen became intrigued with the adaptive turf-tired bike and my stories about teaching children. It was agreed that I would write an article for the Bridgestone Cycling USA Magazine, of which Pedersen was the editor. Pedersen suggested I write an article of about 1,100 words along with a few black and white glossy photographs. Several weeks later, I mailed the draft and photographs to Pedersen. I heard nothing in reply for almost six months, so I literally forgot about having even written the article.

A common complication of Gull's disease is short-term memory loss, which I had been experiencing. Luckily, I could still teach because my subject matter was related to long-term memory, for which I still had adequate retention.

1993. Six months or so went by after the visit with Pedersen. It was now late February or March. A brown envelope arrived rather unexpectedly in the mail. Bridgestone Tire had suffered financial losses in Japan related to the devaluation of the Japanese yen, and Bridgestone had shut down its bicycle operations.

As a consequence, Pedersen was no longer employed by Bridgestone. But because he loved bicycles, he had decided to open his own bike shop in Walnut Creek, California. His newly opened shop published a small rag (a newsletter or "house organ") called *The Rivendell Reader*. The article [20] about my research with teaching children appeared, along with a photograph of my turf-tire trainer. In fact, my article appeared in one of the first issues of Pedersen's publication.

As the story behind the adaptive bike program unfolds, we will again pick up the thread of the Pedersen connection—an unlikely connection that followed events triggered by the obscure 1988 ASME article depicting the precession-cancelling bicycle. When the next connection comes some four years later, the circumstances are equally improbable.

In 1993 the University of Illinois hosted the 100-year anniversary meeting of American Society of Engineering Education (ASEE). I was recruited to display an assortment of my research bikes. Hundreds of visitors came to the event. I recall one curious visitor was the Dean of Engineering from the University of Virginia. Every time he asked a question about bikes, I replied with something like, "Oh, my students and I studied that question X years ago, and the answer is..." After a dozen or so questions and answers, the man stepped back and said, "Klein, you are not being fair." His concern was that I had all this research and yet was not making it available to other researchers, one of the foundational rules in the conduct of science. I have already explained the difficulty in publishing what could be argued to be essentially the work of my students.

By this time, I had become aware that tires, such as turf-style tires, can be mounted in a large lathe and spun. The process allows one to cut rubber away to shape the tire's lateral contour radius. A tire dealership in nearby Royal, Illinois, specialized in this work. The primary clients were Indy 500 race car owners. I took an array of tires to his shop, and the dealer agreed to do them. He liked my work and did the contouring pro bono. That was great, but the drawback was that my work was low on his priorities. It took repeated visits and over a year to get the tires back. These tires were of some value, but I eventually realized that I had to eliminate the need for pneumatic tires altogether.

I was frequently called upon to give presentations of the bicycle project and its findings. I also developed a bedside manner of using magic, or so I claimed, when working with children. Young children found me a large and foreboding figure. One way to alleviate that fear was to adopt a magician's role. Hence, I took to wearing a tall stove pipe hat.

1995. As a professor of the University of Illinois, I was subject to an employee's patent agreement. Subject to this agreement, I submitted a written disclosure of the adaptive bike trainer ideas. After several months of review by the university's attorneys, I was informed that the university had no interest in seeking any patents related to my work.

As part of the research to make a patent ruling, the attorneys for the University of Illinois had come upon a prior patent, US3794351A, of the idea of using a roller as a training adaptation. This patent was granted to Patrick Cudmore of Boston, Massachusetts, dated February 26, 1974 [21]. Cudmore's patent was already in the public domain as his patent and his rights as an inventor had expired. My innovations, beyond Cudmore's, centered on the unique driveline and the introduction of graduated rollers.

The Cudmore U.S. patent of 1974 focused on the use of a crowned roller. The sketches and claims in the patent related to a pedaled device that resembled a tricycle. The rider would propel the vehicle using pedals affixed to the front wheel.

In my application, I used a conventional bicycle frame with a roller replacing the rear wheel. Moreover, my drive train was achieved by incorporating a V-belt drive. The roller was driven by a V-belt that was powered in turn by the rear hub that had been fitted with a V-pulley. As such, I feel that my major innovation dealt with the drive train. Two related innovations were the usage of a series of rollers with varying crowns and the introduction of gearing.

United States Patent [19]

Cudmore

[11] **3,794,351**

[45] **Feb. 26, 1974**

[54] **VELOCIPEDE**

[76] Inventor: **Patrick Cudmore,** 9 Fallon St., Cambridge, Mass. 02138

[22] Filed: **Apr. 24, 1972**

[21] Appl. No.: **246,727**

[52] U.S. Cl. .... 280/204, D34/15 AL, 280/282
[51] Int. Cl. B62k 17/00
[58] Field of Search ... 280/200, 204, 263, 262, 261, 280/282; 34/15 AL, 15 AJ

[56] **References Cited**

UNITED STATES PATENTS

1,375,459	4/1921	Hesse	280/204 UX
2,166,767	7/1939	Petermann	280/11.22
827,012	7/1906	Grove	280/263
2,812,031	12/1957	Aghnides	180/27
2,787,970	4/1957	Bennett	280/259 X
1,797,713	3/1931	Brozelli	280/DIG. 007
3,671,055	6/1972	Aarup	280/87.04 A

FOREIGN PATENTS OR APPLICATIONS

801,891	1/1951	Germany	280/263

Primary Examiner—Kenneth H. Betts
Assistant Examiner—J. M. McCormack
Attorney, Agent, or Firm—Chittick, Thompson & Pfund

[57] **ABSTRACT**

A velocipede having a tractor unit and a detachable semi-trailer unit. The tractor unit includes a front wheel, cranks and foot pedals to drive the front wheel, and a fork and a handlebar to steer the front wheel. The semi-trailer includes a very wide single rear wheel which is shaped like a bulging barrel, and a molded plastic frame which supports the rear wheel and detachably engages the tractor unit fork. The frame has an integral seat formed thereon.

The velocipede is self-stabilizing because its center of gravity (including the rider) is located substantially below the rotational axis of a cone formed in part by the curvature of the rear wheel tread. Therefore, the velocipede is stable like a tricycle at rest and handles like a bicycle when ridden. Furthermore, additional trailer units can be coupled together to form a train behind a single tractor unit.

9 Claims, 5 Drawing Figures

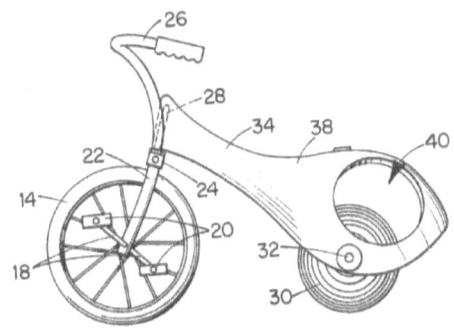

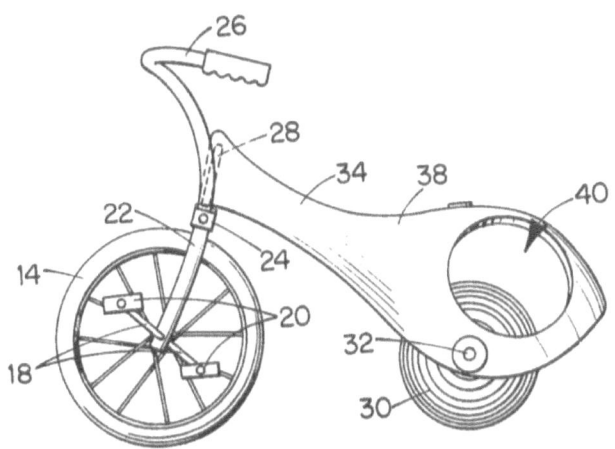

Obtaining and later defending patent protection on such innovations would be challenging at best. The attorneys for the University of Illinois wished me well, signifying that I was free to do whatever I wanted, but it would be on my own nickel and at my own risk. I later came to realize that the University of Illinois seldom pursues patents. A notable exception concerned hybrid seeds as related to agriculture.

From this juncture, I have adopted a policy of not bothering with patents. I am very comfortable with that decision. From my perspective, patents represent a nightmare as well as a money drain. Patents are great for some inventors, especially large corporations, but I prefer to hold my ideas and knowledge close to my chest.

Another objection to patents is the speed of expiration compared to the length of time it takes for an idea to be embraced. Patents expire usually in less than 20 years. To quote a pilot friend, Dr. Andy S. Jones, "It's a long way between the flash and the cash."

Eli Whitney, who invented the cotton gin, died in poverty because numerous mills infringed on his patented idea. Whitney spent large sums trying to recover damages.

A patent is nothing more than a license to sue. One needs a legal budget to bring an action in court. Prior to suing, however, one must become aware of the infringement and find a court of jurisdiction. Then one must prevail in a trial—something less than easy. This is especially true in the case of bicycles, as inventors have tried virtually all conceivable ideas at some prior time. Also, some nations don't honor patents.

Coca Cola® has kept its Coke® recipe secret and thus proprietary for well over a century. In my view, the cost for a competitor to enter the adaptive bicycle trainer market isn't justified since the market is quite small. Frankly, nobody is getting rich teaching kids with disabilities and special needs to master bike riding.

Bikes Go Big Time (1997–2001)

1997. Two significant things happened in March and April 1997. First, some of my students who didn't appreciate my teaching methods and philosophy complained to the head of my department. I met with the department head, and in a surprise move, I submitted my letter of resignation, although he forced my hand.

The benefits of retirement were overwhelmingly in my favor. I discovered that if I retired then I would get about a 20 percent increase in my income. This was in large part because of the quirks of the investment market at the time. During my teaching years (nearly three decades), I had been contributing to a State of Illinois operated retirement account, which in turn was invested in the stock market. Under Illinois law, I was exempted from Social Security as I was covered under the state's retirement plan. The stock market was at a relative high, and I was able to convert my retirement account to a fixed annuity, whose payouts remained locked in for the rest of my life. Any future market corrections would not impact my benefits. By retiring, I substantially increased my take-home income.

As a further incentive for me to retire, the department head sweetened the deal with a "golden parachute," where one gets more benefits by retiring than by remaining on the job. My retirement agreement also stipulated that all bike-related equipment and research bicycles within the University of Illinois would be transferred to my personal possession.

In addition, I was then free to spend my time as I wished. I could not turn that down.

As I sat there facing the department head during that confrontational meeting, I asked him only one question: "Where do I sign?" The complaining students had no idea what a favor they had done for me.

This same department head a few years earlier had asked me, "Why don't you work on wheelchairs?" I chose bicycle research because that's where I saw the challenges and opportunities—not wheelchairs. He had no appreciation for the challenges of the bicycle, but I was firm in knowing what I wanted to do.

Other benefits of retiring at that time accrued. Under state law, my annuity was locked into automatic three percent per annum (compounded) increases. Following my retirement, the state budgets fell on austere times. Three percent was vastly better than any increases I would have received if I had remained on the job.

The retirement package provided me with two things: total freedom in my use of time and ample cash flow to permit me to dive headlong into bicycle activities related to teaching children with disabilities. When I walked out of the building on the University of Illinois campus for the last time, I smiled. I have never looked back, not once.

Within a matter of just a day or two of my meeting with the department head, I received a telephone call from two ladies in Toronto, Ontario. One woman was Laura Hunter. The other woman, Barbara Anthony, had a son in his twenties who was big into biking. The son had shown his mother an old copy of *The Rivendell Reader* from 1993 containing my article [20]. By this time, *The Rivendell Reader* article was equivalent to bird cage lining, yet it caught the eye of these two women. Together, they ran a program in the Toronto area called *Bikes and Balls*. They worked with children with disabilities, affiliated indirectly with what has since become the *Holland Bloorview Kids' Rehabilitation Hospital* in Toronto.

The question Barbara Anthony and Laura Hunter asked was, quite simply, "Can you teach children with disabilities to ride bicycles?" Filled with optimism, I answered, "Yes." I then proceeded to spend the summers of 1997 and 1998 with them in Toronto. This dovetailed perfectly with my retirement agreement, which stipulated that I would spend the academic year of 1997–1998 conducting research off the campus of the University of Illinois. In short, I was so disliked that they didn't even want me to be around.

My work in Toronto was my first introduction to working with children with diagnosed disabilities. To my surprise, the kids—and even teenagers—in Toronto could learn to ride bikes and, in many cases, learn just as quickly as the kids I had worked with back in Illinois. I later realized that some of the children from Illinois must have had issues that had not been diagnosed. Put another way, parents had no need for my services if the child was already riding a bike.

Disabilities come in many forms. Fear immobilizes the body—thus fear itself is a disabling causal factor. The seemingly typical kids whom I had worked with were actually kids with disabilities.

1998. When I traveled to Toronto, the customs people had been rude on both sides of the border. Entry into Canada had been particularly grueling as I was detained for several hours. My van, along with numerous bikes and equipment aboard, was searched with a fine-toothed comb. I was questioned extensively as to my purpose for visiting Canada. I had no documentation with me, as my invitation had been given via undocumented telephone conversations. I was not receiving any pay or reimbursement. I suspect that the Canadian customs assumed I was entering Canada for employment purposes without proper work permit credentials and that I was planning on not paying taxes. My answers to the Canadian customs people were, in their view, beyond plausibility.

As I cleared U.S. customs in Port Huron, Michigan, on my return to Illinois, I was filled with overwhelming joy and incredible sadness. The joy came from my vision of the potential for creating a program that would allow children with disabilities to master bike riding. Yet I was deeply saddened that Barbara Anthony and Laura Hunter could not see this potential. Their inability to share in my dream stemmed from their backgrounds and professional world views. The disparity was rooted in the distinction between two words I touched on earlier: *adapted* and *adaptive*. Their approach to working with children was based on two things: love of the child combined with using adapted equipment. Their adapted equipment included recumbent bikes with three and four wheels. Adaptations in the facility included brightly colored rooms and rooms with soft walls and special lighting. The underlying premise was that the environment would be adapted to suit the needs of the children.

In contrast, I recognized that when on bikes, the ambulatory children were integral to the bikes, and thus part of an adaptive system. I strongly believed that the children, as adaptive systems, could be successful in becoming bike riders on two wheels— without the need for long-term adapted apparatus. Our approaches were worlds apart. Although I gave it my all, my mathematical application of systems theory failed to convince the two ladies.

I will add that the women were focused on a much broader class of children, often with more profound disabilities. In my case, I wanted to serve the class of children who were sighted and ambulatory. I am referring to children with all or most limbs, capable of walking erect without assistive devices. My target population did exclude the more severely disabled, such as children who were quadriplegic and wheelchair-bound.

Crossing the border into the U.S. in August 1998, I reflected on my life as well as my future. That return trip coincided with my official retirement date from the University of Illinois (August 21, 1998). It was then, during the solitude of what I describe as windshield time, that I made a promise both to God and myself to develop a biking program in the United States and to focus on ambulatory children with disabilities.

My vision was to get kids to ride bikes based on a series of specially designed trainers. I later telephoned my Canadian colleagues to ask if they wanted to collaborate. Their answer was a polite but definite "No." The atmosphere I sensed within Bloorview in Toronto was loving but devoid of acceptance of science and mathematics. The Holland Bloorview website to this day has depictions of smiling kids on three and four-wheeled contraptions (that is my word, which is perhaps unkind to their work, but that's how I feel.)

Contraptions do serve a vital purpose for the more profoundly disabled, but there exists a significant segment of children with less severe disabilities who can master bike riding on two wheels given the proper environment—perhaps even 15 percent of the population. My vision focused on the ambulatory child for whom bike mastery had previously been out of reach.

I wish to again bring up the role of fear as an immobilizing factor. Virtually any child who has failed to master bike riding and fears the thought of getting on a bike falls within the definition of being disabled. Given this expansion of what constitutes a child with a disability, the candidate population for the adaptive bike program expands greatly.

I presented at the North American Federation of Adapted Physical Activity (NAFAPA) 1998 Symposium in Minneapolis, Minnesota [22]. I only knew of the conference from a brief conversation with Dr. Patricia Longmuir in Toronto. At the time she was affiliated with a Canadian company that provided equipment for children with disabilities. I met Dr. Longmuir at a facility called Variety Village in Scarborough, Ontario, the township east of Toronto.

An underlying theme in this bike program history is that all sorts of thin chances caused the future to unfold as it did. If it had not been for that chance conversation with Dr. Longmuir, I would probably not have become aware of the Adapted Physical Education (APE) profession. That awareness is what spurred me to collaborate with APE professionals.

For my presentation at NAFAPA in Minneapolis, I brought several trainer bikes and showed some video footage of kids riding. This footage had been taken in 1997 and 1998 in Toronto. I told the audience of about 30 a story about dating in Hawaii. If a maiden in Hawaii is interested and available, she places a flower behind her right ear. If she is not interested or available, she places the flower behind her left ear. I didn't have a flower as I spoke in Minneapolis, but I acted as such. I said that I was seeking to collaborate and that the flower was behind my right ear.

That meeting exposed me, indirectly, to three people who later became involved in the adaptive bicycling activities, albeit to varying degrees. The people were Dr. Pat DiRocco of the University of Wisconsin at La Crosse, Dr. David Poretta of Ohio State University, and Dr. Terry Rizzo of California State University in San Bernardino. Dr. Poretta explained that he had a doctoral student who wished to do a dissertation involving bicycles. I later provided adaptive instruction bikes for Dr. Poretta's student to use in his dissertation studies. The involvements of Dr. DiRocco and Dr. Rizzo will be discussed later.

Another thing I did at the NAFAPA meeting was work the crowd of attendees. I positioned myself in a hallway with my adaptive instruction bikes around me. Although only about 30 people had attended my session, by placing my bikes in a highly trafficked central location, hundreds of meeting attendees stopped to look and ask questions. I soon learned that the Adapted Physical Education profession is much like a dry sponge. The APEs in attendance were looking for something to help them do their job, hopefully as soon as they got back to their schools and kids. In general, they were a curious and easily excited bunch. I knew how to get their attention, and I did.

1999. With the help of an attorney, my wife Marjorie and I formed Rainbow Trainers, Inc., an Illinois corporation. The selection of the name stemmed from the spectrum of colors of the rainbow. We don't teach kids to ride *per se*, but kids will discover how to ride as a consequence of play. I envisioned an array of bikes in graduated colors where each color represented a new level of challenge. By playing on a succession of bikes, kids could and would master bike riding skills. My new corporation, Rainbow Trainers, Inc., remained an unused legal entity until 2004, when it started to conduct business. In 2004, I filed an election with the IRS for the corporation to be treated as an S-Corporation. In tax law jargon, the S-Corporation is treated as a partnership in that the profits and losses, if any, are taxed according to the holders' personal income tax filing obligations. The benefits of an S-Corporation are two-fold: the activities are treated for tax purposes as a partnership and the owners enjoy what is called corporate veil. The purpose of corporate veil is to exempt the personal assets of the owners (like one's home and savings) from any litigation against the corporation. In simple language, it makes it easier to sleep at night.

If we could provide children with designs varying in stability attributes and of different colors, like the rainbow, the children could find the right bike on their own, master it as a form of play, and move on to the next color.

The adaptive bike program as it exists in 2020, the date of this writing, is still founded on the notion of bikes of graduated challenge. The primary differences today are that the staff guide the children in the selection of the level of challenge, and instead of a series of bikes with different speeds or gearing, we now have bikes with multi-gears so switching kids from bike to bike is no longer required.

A small pilot camp was held in La Crosse, Wisconsin, in conjunction with Dr. Pat DiRocco, whom I had met at the NAFAPA conference. The spotters were all APE teachers, whom Dr. DiRocco had invited from the local area. The first camp accommodated three sessions, with four children per session. By then I had accumulated several turf-style bikes. At times the kids outnumbered the available bikes, so we had the kids take turns.

In the photograph above, we see a child on the "Eve" bike, the mother of all later adaptive instruction bikes and roller bikes. That bike was a marvelous workhorse, but it had flaws which became apparent over the many years of its usage. One problem was its heavy weight. When the bike would fall, it could possibly injure the child. Back then, the training handle hadn't yet been incorporated, so a fall usually meant a complete fall.

Below we see yet another modified bike. The turf-style tire on the front was useful in many ways. First, the bike looked easier to ride so kids tended to be more willing to get on. Second, the massive front tire enhanced the gyroscopic component, helping to stabilize the bike. Lastly, the wide tire slowed the fall.

At this point, the reader might be confused regarding the role of the gyroscopic action, or precession, resulting from the rotation of the bicycle's wheels. As the mass or weight of the wheel increases, the precession becomes more pronounced. In my past discussions, I was focused on correcting a longstanding myth about the connection between precession and the ability of a bike to remain upright. Numerous pundits had claimed that the gyroscopic component was the one and only ingredient that made a bicycle remain upright and therefore rideable. I merely proved that the gyroscopic contribution was not indispensable. I did *not* say, however, that the precession exhibited by a rotating wheel was bad or harmful. In fact, the use of a weighted wheel to bolster precession can be quite useful at times.

In the early camps *circa* 1999 to 2002, I had no conventional (two-wheeler) bikes with me when I traveled. Instead, I relied on parents to provide bikes. Unfortunately, those bikes were often inappropriate. Features that we now take for granted, such as training handles and stem risers, as well as properly-designed conventional bikes had not even been thought of yet. So I started bringing my bikes to the camps.

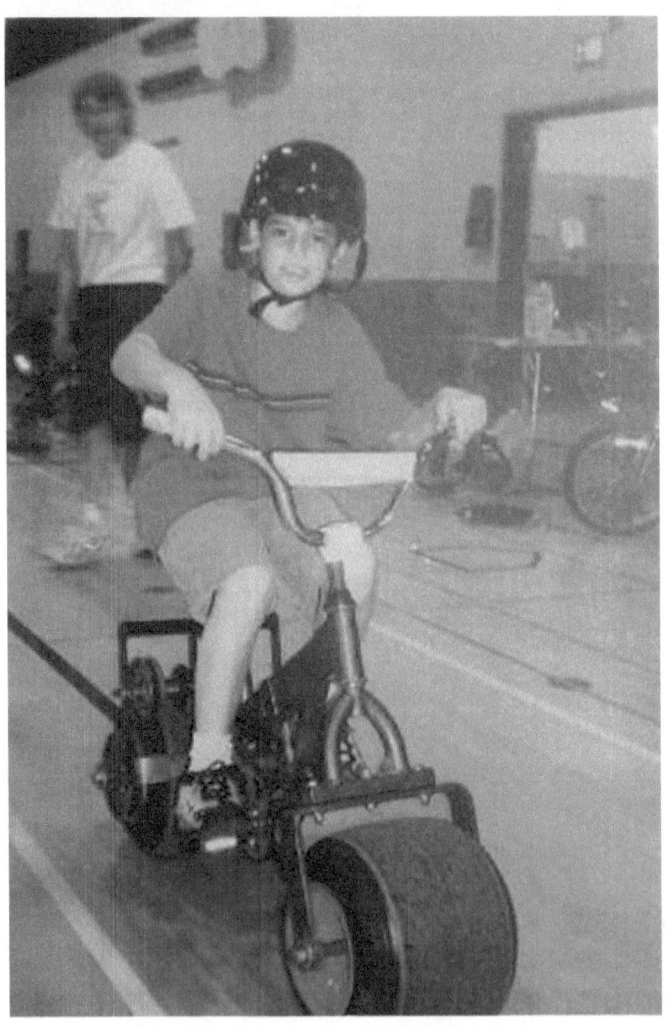

In the photograph above, positioned with a watchful eye behind the child, we see Susan Reimers, Adaptive Physical Educator, from Winters, California.

In the early days I experimented with various kinds of pneumatic tires. The adaptive instruction bike above utilized go-kart racing slicks.

Despite the success of this bike as a lone prototype, mass production was far from easy. For starters, I had a hard time finding a dependable source for the tires. Additionally, the frame was complex and required substantial modifications to accommodate the wide tires. We weren't able to incorporate gearing, and the drivetrain was a nightmare as I had to build in what's called a jackshaft. My best option was to start over and come up with a better overall design.

By this time video recording had become critical. At early camps, I was the tech, the launcher, the spotter, and most everything else. I was so busy that I couldn't watch the tapes until the evening of each day's activities. Marjorie and I would watch the footage for the day and then make informed decisions for the following day's lesson plan for each child.

In the photograph above, Marjorie is running the camera at the camp in La Crosse. I purchased high quality equipment including a professional grade tripod, which allowed us to zoom in and study in detail what each rider was doing. By capturing good footage from the start, watching hour upon hour of recordings was a breeze. And when I wanted to make a video for a presentation, I had clear, steady images that didn't make my audience seasick.

I received a telephone call from Dr. Terry Rizzo in California, whom I had met at the NAFAPA symposium the prior year. He pleaded with me to present at an upcoming APE meeting in California, of which he was program chair. I told Dr. Rizzo, "I am not an APE. It wouldn't be right for me to present at your conference." Dr. Rizzo replied (paraphrased), "Klein, you *are* an APE. You work as an educator with children with disabilities. We (the APE community) are a young profession. We, as a profession, need your training, background, problem-solving skills, and input as an engineer and mathematician." He actually used the term "genetic input" to describe my potential to contribute to the gene pool of ideas within the APE profession and community.

And so I set aside my objections and presented at the meeting [23], in 1999. I also presented again in 2000 [24]. As a result of those two meetings, a camp came about in California in 2001.

In August, while on a trip east to a niece's wedding, I stopped in Warren, Pennsylvania, at Superior Tire & Rubber Company. I met with the engineers and sales staff, and we discussed my needs as I provided specifications for special rollers. The contours were to be cut using computer numerical control (CNC) machining. It was then that I ordered my first set of custom-made rollers. I wanted to try experimenting with a hard roller, one with a low profile. I had concluded that turf-style tires had serious limitations. First, the frame of the bike had to be drastically modified to accommodate the wide and tall tires. Second, the drive train required for a turf-style tire was unwieldy. Third, pneumatic turf tires are not designed with consistent lateral curvature. As such, turf-style tires vary greatly in their cross-sectional shape, so it was not economically feasible to attain consistency. By going to a low-profile roller (having a small diameter), I could use a standard bike frame with minimal modification. The roller, when cut with a groove at the center, allowed me to use a center-line V-belt drive. The matter of consistency, which impacted the bike's tipping rate, was entirely resolved when the solid CNC machined roller became the standard.

2000. A second pilot camp was held in June 2000 in conjunction with Dr. Pat DiRocco. It was while I was in La Crosse for that camp that I stumbled onto my first GT Dyno bike. When I do bike camps I like to visit local bike shops. I purchased a GT Dyno Bazooka model in 16-inch. This bike later became our standard, but I came upon this first one quite by coincidence.

The Adaptive Bike Program Camps Begin (2001–2003)

2001. We held two camps: one in Rohnert Park, California, and one in La Crosse, Wisconsin. In 2001 I switched over to using adaptive instruction bikes with rollers, whereas I had previously used bikes fitted with wide lawnmower-style turf tires.

When planning the camp in California, I had to decide if the future was turf-style bikes or the roller. At that point, the rollers had been tried only once, on a crudely built prototype bike at La Crosse the year before.

I took a leap of faith and shipped rollers to California. I also shipped several boxes of fabricated parts. I ordered a half-dozen GT Dyno bikes from a local bike shop in Cotati, California, close to the camp at Sonoma State University. The six new bikes were waiting for me upon my arrival.

I define our first "camp" as when we started using the adaptive roller bicycles that I had designed and built. The two prior years of pilot camps in La Crosse utilized turf-tire bikes. By using the roller bike as my definition, the first camp held in the United States took place in June 2001 at Sonoma State University in California.

In the photograph above taken in June 2001, I'm preparing to unload the just-purchased GT Dyno Bazooka bikes at a camp supporter's home in Santa Rosa, California. The fleet of bikes was assembled on the Saturday before camp. Assembly required about one hour per roller bike using the parts I had shipped in advance. In later years, the assembly took considerably longer as I added refinements such as chain guards, stem risers, relocated bottom brackets, and gearing. These early roller bikes weren't perfect, but they helped me gain knowledge in how to design and build better bikes. This attitude is reflected in my motto, "Build it wrong, but build it."

When I assembled the roller bikes, the matter of gearing had to be resolved. My decision was to vary the chain rings and rear cogs with different numbers of teeth. Though I built single-speed roller bikes, the bikes had a variation in gears (distance of forward travel per pedal revolution).

After a long work day Saturday, camp started on Monday. The camp at Sonoma State University was a trial balloon. The children had enrolled for the full day, so other activities were scheduled in addition to biking. These activities included swimming, art, and music. Each child rotated through the four sessions of two hours each, with a combined lunch period. When biking, the children were spotted by an APE who had been recruited by the local camp organizer, Dr. Elaine McHugh.

From our perspective, the camp was a success and was appreciated by parents in particular. There was much excitement every time a child mastered riding a two-wheeler. While the overall results were good, not all the children succeeded. Those with more pronounced disabilities had trouble, especially the children with severe cerebral palsy, which limited their ability to pedal fast enough.

It was soon apparent that the adaptive bike program worked better for certain children than for others. The two limiting factors were often either inability to pedal or behavioral issues. When a child refuses to wear a helmet or refuses to get on a bike, that child will not benefit from the program. One can teach biking only if the child can be enticed to try.

As the camp progressed, I made the decision to not ship those first bikes back to Illinois. I had faith that the program would grow, and I didn't want to spend funds moving things needlessly from place to place. A move seldom increases the value of something. I solved the storage problem by loaning out the adaptive instruction bikes to area APEs. I knew that if the bikes were used, the APE teachers would accept the technology and provide me with clinical feedback.

Once back home in Illinois, I fabricated a second set of roller bikes for the camp in La Crosse later that summer.

In these two early camps with roller bikes, the approach was to put kids on bikes geared to their abilities. I would eye the children as they walked in the first day. The hesitant kids were placed on bikes with lower gears. Kids with a faster gait and a more aggressive smile went onto bikes with a somewhat higher gear.

As the children were riding, we effectively switched all kids using a cyclical process. The most advanced child was placed on a bike with a higher gear. This freed up a lower gear bike to which we then promoted another child. We would eventually "bump up" all children when a change in gearing was warranted. Because we were switching kids from bike to bike, we were required to do many seat changes and sometimes handlebar changes or adjustments. Now that we have bikes with multiple gears, we just flick a lever and the bike has been changed to suit that child's needs.

I presented a paper in Vienna, Austria, at the International Symposium of Adapted Physical Activity in July, 2001 [25]. From my perspective, there seemed to be scant interest. However, I did meet Dr. Dale Ulrich of the University of Michigan. I asked if he would be interested in doing something with the bike program, possibly as a research topic. He was polite, but gave no hint of commitment. It was not until several years later that something did actually come of this encounter.

Marjorie and I drove to Montreal, Canada in the late summer. Our sole purpose was to meet with Dr. Greg Reid, then president of the International Adapted Physical Activity Federation. I asked him what the process would be for the APE profession to become aware of the adaptive bike program and if, at some point, they would start to get involved with it. He replied that the process was slow and that if I would continue to give presentations and make it visible, the profession would eventually embrace it.

Around 2001, a friend, Dean Rothermel, introduced me to a machinist, Steve Smith, willing to do custom work for my bike activities. Steve's work was exemplary, and he became an essential element in the creation of the adaptive instruction bike fleets. Even as I write this almost two decades later, Steve remains my primary vendor for building bikes. As an example of his work, Steve is the one who constructs the tandem bike frames, all of which are from a design I provided him.

2002. We conducted three camps: La Crosse, Wisconsin; Rohnert Park, California; and Davis, California. The camp in Davis happened due to the efforts of Susan Reimers, APE from Winters California, who had been at the first camp at Sonoma State University in 2001.

2003. The program continued to grow as we held eight camps.

One camp was held in Fond du Lac, Wisconsin. It was there that I had interactions with two medical professionals. Dr. Elliot Phillips had enrolled his son, age 10 at the time, and observed the camp. Dr. Phillips was board-certified in sleep medicine. He introduced me to several important medical implications of sleep, the most notable being that humans learn and refine certain motor skills, including bike riding, during REM sleep. This is important because it provides the foundation and justification for conducting our camps over a string of days, as well as our sufficiency with 75-minute sessions. Longer or additional sessions in the same day prove to be counter-productive.

The second medical professional was Dr. Darrell Treffert of Fond du Lac. Dr. Treffert, who specializes in Savant syndrome, is a leading specialist in autism. The movie *Rain Man* (1988) starring Dustin Hoffman came about because of Dr. Treffert, who also served as medical consultant to the script and the movie. Dr. Treffert and I had discussions regarding the importance of the adaptive bike program as a means of providing therapy for children diagnosed with autism spectrum disorder (ASD). He repeatedly said "Klein, get ready." His point was that a day would come when the demand for the program would be gigantic.

By this time the GT Dyno bikes had become my standard. I had also added numerous GT Dyno Blaze model bikes in 20-inch wheel size. It was at that point, unfortunately, that GT Dyno filed for bankruptcy. The parent company in Europe collapsed, so that brought down GT Dyno as well. I was in a jam. I purchased GT Dyno Bazooka and Blaze bikes whenever I could find them in stores. I purchased six Blaze bikes in Columbus, Ohio, and another six in Milwaukee, Wisconsin. For a span of years, I added more GT Dyno bikes when I could buy them used on Internet listings. Sadly, one cannot build a national program on bikes that are no longer being produced. Coming up with a new workhorse became an issue.

Marjorie and I moved from Champaign County, Illinois, to the St Louis area. On March 9, 2003, we held a public auction at our farm in Dewey, Illinois. The auctioneer started at 10 a.m. and wrapped up at 4 p.m. He sold, on average, one lot or item every 30 seconds. I estimated that I got rid of about 70,000 pounds of stuff.

I purchased the 735 Park Drive commercial building in Alton, Illinois, in December 2003 to use for the Rainbow Trainers program.

To help with the move from Champaign to St. Louis, I purchased a used, but serviceable, enclosed cargo trailer. I then used that trailer to haul bikes to and from bike camps, excluding the West Coast area. Now that I had adequate carrying capacity, I could bring conventional bikes to the camps as well as adaptive roller bikes. The days of depending on parents for conventional bikes came to an end. We still used family-provided bikes but only after the children had mastered the two-wheelers I provided.

At the Easter Seals camp in Villa Park, Illinois, we started using floor supervisors. Previously, each spotter, typically an APE, functioned as his/her own supervisor. Now, for the first time, teenage volunteers were the spotters instead of APEs and Special Education teachers.

Three of us—Marjorie, Laura Znada, and myself—stood in the middle of the floor and together became the floor supervisor. We had different backgrounds, but as a team we complemented each other well. Marjorie was a trained educator (having taught kindergarten for 42+ years), Laura was a physical therapist, and I functioned as the bike guru. We would discuss the children, and we learned from each other how to better direct each child on a case-by-case basis. Our statistics improved, and I soon realized that we were better as a team than any individual spotter.

As camps continued and the program evolved, I realized what made the program successful, and, in a complementary sense, why the parents could not compete with us. The missing ingredient for most parents is the knowledge of how to properly coach the child so that the child can discover how to master balancing and bike riding. Remember that bike riding isn't something we teach a person to do, it is a discovered skill. Also, being able to balance while pedaling is a binary event: you can either do it or you can't. Being able to ride a bike happens in a flash—almost akin to popcorn popping.

Each child will ultimately discover how to ride a bike as long as the environment is conducive for that discovery. Three things make up what I deem to be the proper environment: an appropriate bike, a good location, and the right spotting method. What defines the best spotting method is complex to outline in a few sentences, much like achieving a good golf swing or diving like Esther Williams is not easily put into words. The spotter's guiding hand can't be too much or too little. Most inexperienced spotters tend to use too much hand. A child will never master bike riding as long as the spotter is hanging on. The guiding hand and reassuring voice must be carefully measured.

The Adaptive Bike Program Continues (2004–present)

OVER THE NEXT FEW YEARS, I was approached by several established national charities, including Easter Seals, Make-A-Wish Foundation, the Lance Armstrong Foundation, and another charity that I suspected to be the Hole in the Wall Gang, initially created by movie actor Paul Newman. In all cases, after some discussions the charities said well done, but that the mission statements did not properly dovetail. I realized then that if a charitable group became involved, it would have to be a charity dedicated to the support and delivery of the adaptive bike program.

As the program expanded, so did the problems. One critical issue concerned my personal liability. If a child were ever seriously injured, I would likely be named in a lawsuit. At the time, I had no insurance. I worked for free. Because I was engaged in charitable activities, I reasoned that my homeowner's insurance policy covered me.

Being a volunteer, my cash outlay grew with each camp that was added to the schedule. At one point, my children sensed that their inheritance was being squandered. I reminded them that no law or even Biblical code required me to pass wealth onto my children. But to keep peace in the family, I agreed that I would henceforth do camps only if my out-of-pocket expenses, such as hotels, travel, and meals, were reimbursed. I did not charge for my time or for the use of the equipment. Today, the insurance and liability problems still exist, but they are at least contained.

As a designer, builder, and provider of special bikes used by children with known disabilities, it's close to impossible to get an underwriter to even give me a quotation. Feeling frustrated, I once posed this question to an insurance agent: "If I was willing to pay $1 million in annual premium for a policy with $1 million in coverage, would your company write me such a policy?" To my astonishment, the agent replied, "No." The point is that this activity is not clean. There is no statistical basis for an actuary to determine a premium. As such, the risks are too dirty for the underwriting company to even want to become involved.

2004. We held 14 camps. The growth in the program was sparked due to articles in *Midwest Living* [26] and in the University of Illinois alumni magazine [27]. Because of the articles about teaching children, I started to get an increasing number of telephone calls and emails from parents. I decided to provide as much information as I could on my website to save my own time while still helping others. I needed to focus on building more and better equipment, as well as getting my new facility in Alton, Illinois, up and functioning. I couldn't be repeating the same information over and over on the phone and in emails.

Some people said my website was poor and wasn't user friendly. I had planned it with precisely that intent. Only the serious could navigate through it. I had more demand for camps than I could possibly fill, so my goal was not marketing or expansion. Instead, my goal was to do some camps and in doing so, improve the equipment and the way camps were done. I was focused on designing bikes, gaining clinical experience, and developing an infrastructure.

The University of Illinois strives to keep in touch with its former students. Many graduates receive the *Illinois Alumni* magazine. My work with bicycles and children with disabilities was the subject of one article called "Rollers and the Renaissance Man" in the March/April 2004 issue [27]. A former student, Mary, from the fall semester of 1982, was inspired to contact me. She was married, had a child, and was working and living in New Jersey. Mary marveled about how uniquely God had touched our respective lives. She had a child with a disability, so the topic of getting her child to ride a bike deeply affected her. Recall that Mary, with her father's professional assistance, authored the first student essay in January of 1983 attempting to explain how and why a bike works. Her essay was pivotal as an impetus for the bike research at the University of Illinois. She had been at ground zero, and now some 22 years later the program had the potential to impact her child and herself personally. I have been asked if Mary's child ever attended one of our camps, but I do not know that specific answer.

I became increasingly aware of the theology of bike riding. I composed what I call sermonettes wherein I comment on how bike riding relates to faith and even certain scripture passages. In my view, learning to ride a bike boils down to faith. Those with strong faith will succeed. Those with little faith tend to struggle. Later in this book, I will come back to biking and faith.

2005. Dr. Dale Ulrich, University of Michigan, embarked on a multi-year study of the benefits of riding bikes for children with Down syndrome. Dr. Ulrich and I collaborated, and my adaptive bikes were central to his research. His later studies expanded to include children with a diagnosis of autism spectrum disorder (ASD). Dr. Ulrich, in conjunction with several of his graduate students, has since published their findings. In summary, the research at the University of Michigan [28] yielded several major conclusions:

1. Children with Down syndrome, upon learning to ride and upon retaining that skill, have an appreciable reduction in B.M.I. (body mass index).

2. These children also, based on a 14-month follow-up, show a decrease in sedentary activity of approximately 75 minutes per day. This finding has considerable significance, as the children aren't necessarily riding a bike for 75 minutes every day. Rather the children who master and retain bike riding skills are more active overall.

3. The level of parental expectation rises dramatically. This applies to all children involved in the study, including those who did not master and retain bike riding skills.

4. Skill retention can be increased significantly when some form of organized follow-up is provided after each camp. In the Ulrich study, this amounted to having the children and parents return for weekly riding sessions each Saturday for approximately eight weeks. The University of Michigan provided suitable bicycles, college-aged spotters, and an appropriate place to ride.

We held 18 camps in 2005. The first dual tandem trainer of my manufacture was put into service. The initial reason for the tandem was to make it easier for the spotter, hence less running. It has since been found that the tandem yields certain important benefits:

1. The children can experience the "wind in the face" and the joy and smoothness of bike riding.

2. The tandem ride becomes a valuable diagnostic tool.

3. The children usually like the tandem ride. This can be used as a reward for getting back on the roller bike.

4. The tandem ride can loosen children up. Beginning or fearful riders are often tense and ride with rigid bodies. The coach in the rear position can superimpose a high

frequency oscillation or wiggle onto the handlebars. The wiggling, which is known as a dither in systems theoretic terminology, will cause something that acts stiff to become looser. For example, if cereal won't flow out of the box, a little shaking of the box will change that.

Also in 2005, *Bicycling Magazine* carried a feature article about the program and my bike activities [29].

2006. In order to meet the growing demand, I built a third fleet for the West Coast. The other two fleets served the central part of the country and East Coast. In 2006, I purchased two additional cargo-style enclosed trailers: one for the West Coast fleet and a second for the Midwest, bringing the total trailer count to three. Now that I had so much equipment, I needed to consider standardization. Consistency makes it easier to service the fleets and is also helpful for the staff using the fleets.

We held 33 camps that year. It was also the year that the first roller bikes with gearing were introduced.

In the fall, I talked with the Down Syndrome Association of Sweden about possibly doing a camp in Stockholm in 2007. But a Swedish national election that fall changed the funding picture and the idea of a camp in Sweden faded away. I have since come to the view that expanding into Europe will be hard. The culture is vastly different, and the economies are strongly socialistic. The only charity with any clout in most European countries is the government with its coffers of tax money. Unfortunately, those funds characteristically get directed to causes based on politics. Those entities already getting funding are not likely to step aside for some upstart program. Politics control the flow of money, so if you aren't connected with politics don't expect to get too big a slice or any slice at all.

2007. The national charity Lose the Training Wheels, Inc. (LLTW Inc.) was founded. Certain key parents and host advocates had begun discussions at a camp in Danville, Illinois, in the summer of 2006. A dinner meeting was held at the quaint Possum Trot restaurant on the outskirts of Danville with the expressed purpose of creating a national charity. John Lord of Virginia (parent), Pete Blackmon of Danville (camp host), Dan Hennessey also from Danville (assistant camp host), Lou Ann Carver (parent) from Colorado, and myself as founder of Rainbow Trainers, Inc., participated in the discussion. Several others may have been present, but my memory can't bring any more names back.

We all understood that a national charity was needed so that the program could expand beyond the limits of what I could do personally. John Lord took on the task of finding an attorney *pro bono* to draft the articles of incorporation in Virginia, where we decided to base the organization. Once the corporation was created, we applied to the IRS for status as a 501(c)3 charity. In late spring of 2007, LLTW, Inc. officially assumed operations of camps in both the United States and Canada.

The charity hired a full-time CEO in 2007: Mr. Matt Hampton of Wichita, Kansas. Later in 2007 an anonymous corporate donor contributed substantial funding to provide a salary and overhead expenses for Mr. Hampton. The donor insisted that their name and the terms of the donation not be disclosed. That donation was for a multi-year period but has since expired. I will say that the donor was a major national corporation and that the corporation was not in any way associated with the bicycle business. By contract, Rainbow Trainers, Inc. became the supplier of adaptive instruction bikes and related equipment to the LTTW Inc. charity. To date, the national charity is the sole user of the equipment provided by Rainbow Trainers, Inc.

We held 37 bike camps.

2008. We held 52 camps, including three camps in British Columbia.

2010. I presented my bike research at an international bicycle-related symposium in Delft, Netherlands [30]. More than 100 researchers in bicycle and motorcycle theory and practice attended. There was little interest in teaching children to ride bikes, much less children with disabilities. I again realized that the cultural differences were great. The Dutch, for example, as a society refuse to wear helmets. When I asked about Dutch children with disabilities, I got mostly blank stares. It seemed that these Dutch researchers didn't admit that children in their population had disabilities.

My sense was that, worldwide, most serious bicycle and motorcycle researchers follow the money. The money comes from a limited number of sources: the motorcycle industry, based largely in Japan, and high-end bike manufacturers with a focus on racing.

2011. In August 2011, Marjorie and I purchased the commercial building at 1480 Pearl Street in Alton, Illinois. A massive renovation was undertaken. The photos below show the work of tearing off the building's rotted roof and then the placement of new trusses.

After the trusses were set in place, the structure was then encapsulated with a modern steel roof.

The acquisition of the adjacent second building in Alton was a significant step forward. The larger commercial building afforded many advantages, including the ability to receive freight and another adequate secure indoor parking area for trailers in the off-season.

2012. Marjorie and I formed a separate corporation, Rainbows End Cyclery, Inc., which functioned as a retail bike shop. Its purpose was to allow RTI direct access to a retail supplier of bikes and assorted bike parts.

Now I finally had the ability to open wholesale accounts with several major bike parts suppliers. Also, as a retail bike shop owner, I was able to obtain the necessary sales tax numbers that go along with a retail business. Please note that while I operate a retail bike shop, I service only one customer: my other corporation, Rainbow Trainers, Inc. My bike shop, at least at this point, keeps no regular hours.

The national charity underwent a change in leadership, marketing philosophy, and name, becoming iCanShine, Inc. Lisa Ruby and Jeff Sullivan assumed command. During the previous season in 2011, I had attended only one bike camp, one out of 73. It was at that camp near Philadelphia that Jeff Sullivan and I became acquainted. Jeff strongly believes that our chance meeting in 2011 was far more than pure luck. Other chances also played a role in bringing Jeff Sullivan onto the charity's leadership team, but I will leave it for Jeff to write his own narrative.

I produced a dual tandem trainer of a new design in 2012. This new design featured a drag link as opposed to a connecting chain for the rear steering action. The connecting chain for pedaling has no idler, but rather the front bottom bracket shifts forward and tightens the chain. The rear steer stem assembly is vastly stouter and can be removed, making shipping in a standard carton feasible.

2016. During the summer of 2016, iCanShine utilized 13 operational fleets. In addition, the infrastructure supporting the program was sound. Production of new adaptive instruction bikes had become standardized and used standard parts. Vendors were in place and equipped to provide parts, both those commercially available as well as proprietary parts of my design. The 1480 Pearl Street property had been transformed into a secure building with large overhead doors. All of our fleet trailers could now be parked inside that building when not engaged in active camps. Rainbow Trainers, Inc. even had additional adaptive instruction bikes made for a standby fleet.

We conducted approximately 90 camps in 2016 and another 90 in 2017.

Prior to the 2016 season, I designed, assembled, and introduced a new line of cruiser bikes that could be used selectively as fixed wheel drives as well as free wheel drives. We dubbed these new bikes "Fixies. "Each year I continue to make improvements and innovations in the composition of the fleets. Each year it seems we do more and more camps. And each year we get to see the smiling faces of children feeling the wind in their face as they discover how to ride a bike.

AS EASY AS RIDING A BIKE

WITH THE HISTORY of the adaptive bike program established, let's now dive into some topics and issues as they relate to bicycles.

Bikes Fall Six Different Ways

BIKES COMMONLY FALL for one of six distinct reasons (apart from trying stunts like wheelies or airborne competition riding). By knowing what to look for, it's possible to intervene and prevent the fall.

Here are the six usual ways that bikes fall, along with the associated intervention strategy:

Cause #1: Crashing into something. The bike and rider crash into something like a curb, tree, or parked car, or encounter another issue like a soft surface, uneven surface, or drainage grate. In other words, the riding surface is no longer conducive to bike riding.

Intervention: Our business is to get kids to ride bikes on flat and suitable surfaces. The rider must be taught to recognize road hazards and to avoid them by stopping or maneuvering around them.

Cause #2: Wiping out. Wipe-out is the sudden lateral (sideways) sliding action of one or both tires on the riding surface. One common cause is excessive speed when turning, which leads to an excessive angle of lean. The lateral friction limits, which act between the tire (or tires) and the riding surface, are exceeded. Another typical cause is when the rider comes onto a riding surface with loose sand, gravel, oil, grease, or water. Once a wipe-out starts, there's little chance the rider will recover, especially if the front tire wipes out first. A wipe-out comes suddenly and without warning.

Intervention: The best remedy is to ride cautiously and to be alert to such hazards. In the bike program, if new riders are going too fast, we simply ask them to slow down. If that doesn't work, we direct them to do serpentines or figure eights within a marked rectangular area to diminish the tendency to hot-dog at high speeds.

Cause #3: Excessive braking, causing wheel lock-up. A variation of the wipe-out scenario results when the rider applies the brakes excessively. Having the front wheel lock up is particularly serious because the rider may be unable to make steering corrections. When the rear wheel locks up due to a braking action, the more skilled riders can often recover and regain stability.

Intervention: The vast majority of bikes used within our program have brakes only on the rear wheel.

Cause #4: Capsizing. Bikes will sometimes capsize. This is a rolling motion, often slow, in one direction. The most frequent cause is that the rider is too stingy with steering or is riding with locked and fixed elbows. It can also occur when a rider turns modestly but slowly. This usually happens when a novice rider approaches a wall or the end of the riding area. Because they are afraid or uncertain, they slow their pedaling. The bike and rider tend to go into an inward spiral. The spiral happens as the handlebars are turned into the fall but not far enough. Another cause of capsizing is when novice riders are fixated on what we call shoulder shifting. Shoulder shifting (or upper torso articulation) is a common symptom of riders who have previously relied on training wheels.

Intervention: For the first two causes of capsizing, I recommend that the spotter use their open palm to push the bike to increase its speed. This will subsequently cause an increase in the *centripetal forces* associated with turning. (Many refer to this as a *centrifugal* force; however, the word *centrifugal* stems from the Latin roots meaning "the fugitive who is fleeing from the center" [from justice]. So using the term *centrifugal* force for this concept is incorrect.) Technically speaking, the *centripetal force* is the force exerted by the riding surface that opposes the sliding action of the tire. To prevent capsizing from shoulder shifting, we have developed intervention techniques to eliminate the urge for shoulder shifting. For example, the spotter can gently lean the bike in the direction of the shift as soon as the rider begins to shift their shoulders to one side. Our intervention techniques are sophisticated and require a bit more explanation than what can be stated here in a few sentences. If your rider is often capsizing, and especially if you notice shoulder shifting, consider enrolling the child in one of the adaptive bike camps. Our specialized bikes and trained spotters are equipped to phase out shoulder shifting and eventually extinguish it from the rider's motor plan.

Cause #5: Weaving. The bike and rider will go into a weave mode that tends to grow in amplitude. The presence of the weave mode tells us that the rider has a proper motor plan for riding a bike. The difficulty is rooted in two causes: the mental processing is delayed so the rider's corrective steering actions are likewise delayed, and the rider is overcorrecting.

Intervention: Whenever we observe a weave pattern in riding, we know that success is close at hand. It is only necessary for the spotter to continue to run with the child. As long as the child remains upright, the weave will often transition into a stable weave. Soon the rider will master bike riding.

A zig-zag ride is expected, normal, and should not be interfered with. Many spotters, upon observing a zig-zag riding pattern, incorrectly try to hold onto the training handle—but this is detrimental as it greatly slows down and at times destroys the rider's adaptive processing. Once the rider has demonstrated the tendency to turn into the direction of fall, it is vastly better to let go of the training handle. That seemingly precarious zig-zag will disappear in mere minutes provided the spotter can resist the temptation to save the child by trying to intervene. During the zig-zag, the rider is engaging in a pattern recognition process. It is critical that the rider be allowed to put cause and effect together.

Another option for dealing with the weave mode would be more time on the dual-steered tandem trainer or more time on an adaptive roller training bike. Over the years we have developed an expression: "Let the roller do the work." It's a mistake to take the child off the roller bike too soon. Some argue that the child seemed ready for launch on a two-wheeler, but what's the hurry? The roller bikes were designed for a specific reason. Yes, children can be launched earlier but that early launch requires an increase in the time running behind a child.

Cause #6: Front Wheel Wobbling. Front wheel wobble involves a modestly high frequency oscillation of the front fork and front wheel assembly. Front wheel wobble rarely happens in bicycles. It's an issue of minimal concern, especially when the rider's hands remain on the handlebars. The closest thing to wobble in a bicycle would be when a rider suddenly swerves the front fork, causing the bike to go down.

Intervention: The new rider who yanks around on the handlebars needs to go back to a roller bike with a low-numbered (flatter) roller. Children and riders who exhibit radical steering, almost to the point of being uncorrelated to the bicycle's leaning and turning, are focused on a motor plan that is counterproductive and often does not involve feedback as to what the bike is telling the rider.

My experience suggests that the root cause of such erratic steering behavior is that the child's creative mind has invented a mental picture of what to do when riding a bike. But this invention is often not based in reality. This situation is perhaps the most difficult to correct. Riders with a flawed and invented motor plan do have a motor plan, albeit improper. The best solution is to extinguish the faulty motor plan by replacing it with an improved one. Unfortunately, the child is prone to holding onto the delusionary plan while being oblivious to reality, despite intervention attempts.

I've also seen cases where the delusionary child pretends that he or she can ride a bike. One such child created the impression that he could ride and went to the effort to leave a bike (with no training wheels) parked conspicuously at his home so as to be visible in the driveway. Peers and neighbors assumed he could ride a bike, but nobody ever got to see him ride it.

Cats, Dogs, and Bike Riding

WHEN WE RIDE A BIKE, an incredible harmony exists, and *must* exist. All parts of the rider's body, as well as the parts of the bike, act in harmony.

In aerospace engineering parlance, we jest saying that the "tail wags the dog." If any part of an aircraft flexes and wiggles, that movement is shared by all parts of the aircraft. This means that each part is connected and working in unison with all other parts. The motion of any one component isn't an isolated happening. It is not customary for the dog to wag its tail without each and every other part of the entire body wagging in response. In this sense, a dog wagging its tail is a mechanism.

Does the dog wag its tail, or does the tail wag the dog? It really is one and the same because one can't occur without the other being true. The dog and the tail are connected—parts of the same body—and act in unison.

In contrast, a perched cat might twitch its tail, but only the tail moves. The rest of the body of the cat is rigid, cemented in place to wherever the cat is standing or sitting. In engineering terms, the cat's body as a whole is a "structure," something quite different from a mechanism. Yes, the tail might move, but it is only the tail that moves relative to a structure that is held rigid.

Bicycles in motion are analogous to dogs, in that every motion of any part of the bicycle, including its rider, will cause sympathetic and simultaneous motions in all the other parts. The dog's entire body acts as a mechanism, with all parts acting in collaboration. Similarly, the bicycle and rider in motion act as a mechanism.

Tricycles and bicycles with training wheels, in stark contrast, are actually rigid structures. The outrigger wheels prevent sway of the frame. Because the frame can't sway, it can't move in response to motions of the other parts, notably the front fork or the rider's body leans. In essence, tricycles and bikes with training wheels act like cats, whereas bicycles (those with just two wheels) act like dogs.

When fearful children are trying to learn to ride bikes, they frequently adopt behaviors similar to cats. They will only move one limb or do a small shoulder-shift.

Children with motor problems can benefit from equestrian therapy, as the horse is dog-like: fluid and moving. Therapy with dolphins yields similar benefits. The developmentally challenged rider on a horse is able to acquire some of the horse's fluidity. In both the cases of horses and bicycles, once the rider is successful, they improve their motor balance at a surprisingly rapid rate. Conversely, a child using training wheels will often make stingy progress. But when that same child is placed on our horse-like adaptive instruction bikes, the motor learning proceeds at an astounding rate.

Becoming a successful bike rider ultimately requires that the rider act in a fluid manner, so as to become one with the bike.

Five Observations About the Program

EVEN AS A PERSON WITH NO TRAINING in disabilities or related therapy methods, five things continue to amaze me:

1. Our methodology works for children with a wide array of disabilities.
2. The speed at which the kids are able to master bike riding is counted in hours, not years, months, or even weeks. Some parents have worked for up to 10 years to get their child to ride, but we commonly do it in a few hours or a few days.
3. The size of the population that can benefit from this program—and the potential for impacting lives—remains immense.
4. The families are profoundly grateful. Getting hugged is a risk that comes with this profession. The lyrics of the Gershwin musical come to mind: "Nice work if you can get it." I can say that in my 30 years of dealing with engineers, I never once saw a tear or heard a thankful sigh. Indeed, the pay scale for what I do is low, but the retirement plan in heaven is something that is out of this world.

5. While the bike activity falls within what most would classify as adapted physical activity, there is a striking distinction. In writing about the creation of a bike program, I have been steadfast in using the adjective *adaptive*—not *adapted*. The adaptive bike program utilizes adaptive equipment. The adaptive bike program enables the child to master a skill—in this case riding a two-wheel bicycle. Once the child acquires the skills and their brain becomes wired correctly, they are elevated to a position on par with their non-disabled peers. The child is transformed. In comparison, most adapted physical activities dumb down the activity and the child remains largely unchanged. In fact, it is not uncommon for a child with a disability who goes through our program to outperform their peers at bike riding.

I know of few other adapted physical activities that share this attribute, much less with such a short and dramatic learning process. Yes, horses and dolphins serve many people with disabilities, but bicycles are easier to have at home. Horses and dolphins have to be fed and cared for. The child has to be transported to the horse or dolphin. In the vast number of cases, equestrian and dolphin therapies need to be repeated over and over. In stark contrast, the child is involved in our program only as long as it is required to master the biking skills. Once the child masters these skills, they are done with the program!

New Bike!

As I spent decades working with children, I came to realize that silence is golden. I developed the approach of using economy of language. By design, I would sequence children through a succession of bikes. The few words spoken at the start of each step simply boiled down to "New bike!" As I said those words, I would also use my hand and pat the seat gently. The children became accustomed to getting on each successive bike based on those two promptings.

When the time came for the final and ultimate launch, I would act as if this new bike was just another step. I would signify my request for the child to get on this last bike with a gentle patting gesture on the bike's seat along with the then familiar words "New bike." The child would invariably get on and be successful in riding. I feel that the phrase "New bike!" cleanly embodies the essence of the program.

Because I interacted with children with varied disabilities, I became aware of the needs of children with hearing loss. I considered becoming fluent in American Sign Language. Upon making inquiries, I was advised to not pursue this aspect of professional development. Knowledgeable colleagues made three points:

1. The time for me to learn American Sign Language would be better devoted to the development and production of additional adaptive instruction bikes.

2. The needs of children with hearing loss could be served by those already fluent in ASL.

3. Because I was immersed with children with hearing losses, I had already become accustomed to the basics of ASL. Patting the bike seat meant, "new bike, get on." I indicated "Put your helmet on" by demonstrating putting an imaginary helmet on my head. I communicated "pedal the bike" by pedaling my hands. In short, I was already fluent in the basics as pertained to biking.

So I left ASL to the professionals and stuck with my own familiar language: "New bike!"

Trading Problems

WHEN TALKING WITH PARENTS at the start of a bike camp, I typically delivered my standard line: "The problem is that their child cannot *yet* ride a bike." The goal of the camp was to solve that problem.

However, a new problem would soon replace the first—their child *could* ride a bike. I would then reassure them that the second problem was preferable to the first.

With that background in hand, here are some stories from across the years.

One particular boy in California had an aversion to wearing a helmet. This boy had a weakness—he liked popsicles. The plan was simple. If he wanted a popsicle, he had to wear his helmet. He would put the helmet on, gobble down the popsicle, and immediately tear the helmet off. After a year of this, he was able to wear a helmet. He learned to ride a bike.

At bike camps, as children go through puberty and beyond, sometimes love is in the air. Boys, such as those with Down syndrome, can become interested in camp staff. Marriage proposals have been uttered. One practical response is, "Fred, I really appreciate the marriage proposal—but I can't consider it until you can ride a bike."

A girl in California was constantly falling off her roller bike. We soon realized that she was falling off the bike on purpose. Her spotter was a handsome male college student. Each time she fell off, Prince Charming scooped her up in his arms. We solved the problem. We replaced Prince Charming with a less attractive frog.

A boy in New York, after attending bike camp and learning to ride, started riding his bike off the front porch. The parent asked for suggestions. The suggestion was simple: Purchase a mountain bike with suspension.

A boy with Down syndrome in Michigan mastered bike riding. At home following camp, the boy arose one morning. He found some money in the house, then while his parents were still sleeping, took off on his bike. He rode a mile or so to a fast food establishment and bought some food. The boy then returned home, again on his bike. The parents were awakened as the boy came into their bedroom to serve them breakfast in bed. The father later remarked that he wanted some independence for his son—but not quite *that* much.

When I was in Toronto in 1997 working for the first time with kids having diagnosed disabilities, there was a girl about age nine. In fact, as I recall, she was my first attempt at launching a child with a known disability. I don't recall the specific issue, but let's assume it was autism spectrum disorder. She had been riding her bike, then fitted with training wheels. Again, this was way before my creation of adaptive roller trainers. I removed the training wheels. Then, with few words I launched her. To my astonishment, and obviously hers, she rode the bike all the way across the gymnasium floor. Without being told, she braked, came to a stop, and got off. She then put the kickstand down. Her next move astonished me once again. She beelined it back to me and with considerable tone in her voice and facial expression, to the point of consternation, blurted out, "Doctor Dick! Why didn't you tell me it was easy to ride a bike?" I later informed the girl's mother that her child was now a bike rider. The mother's reply was "No way." The mother didn't believe it until she saw her daughter ride. I learned one rule that I follow to this day: I am steadfast in telling all children that riding a bike is easy.

In Wisconsin a boy, age 10, came to one of our camps. The boy had a congenital birth defect. One leg stopped at the middle of his thigh. The other leg stopped at mid-calf. The boy mastered bike riding! I'm talking about a conventional bike—not some contraption with lots of side wheels and outriggers. That boy was such an inspiration. After he mastered bike riding, he then turned his attention to assisting and encouraging others. He said to one struggling girl, a girl with a dual diagnosis of autism spectrum disorder and Down syndrome, "Angie, everything is possible as long as you try."

I know that God's hand has been at work as He has blessed the adaptive bike program and me personally.

When kids discover the joy that comes with bike riding, they often express it as a succinct declaration: "I can't get enough!" Or in the example of a one boy, "It's not the same." He was expressing how different his world had become once he transitioned to being a bike rider. His world had been turned upside down: It wasn't the same.

These are all "problems" I'm happy to live with.

One Personal Story of Emotional Impact

WITHOUT QUESTION, I could fill volumes recounting the personal stories of the many children and families affected by the bike program. I will share one story that is deeply personal and touching. In fact, whenever I try telling the story in public, I find it hard to hold back my tears.

In California, a girl about age 12 had participated in the program and mastered riding a bike. As was my usual custom, I proceeded to ask the child's mother if she would go riding with her daughter.

She answered, "No, but her father will." I asked why she wasn't going as well. She said simply, "I don't know how to ride a bike."

As I recall, it was late morning on a Thursday. I suggested she drive to her nearby home, change into clothing more suitable for riding, and then come back. Over the lunch hour that day I worked with her. After progressing through a few of our rollers, I launched her on a conventional adult-sized bike. She was riding a bike for the first time in her life. The total time between starting and mastery was about 30 minutes. Once she had mastered it, I went about my affairs, tending to other things as usual.

Nobody noticed that she was gone. About half an hour later, a lady went into the restroom and discovered our new rider crying out of control. When asked what was wrong, the whole story came out.

When she was around 12 years old, her father bought her a new bike. It was one of those 1970s-era road bikes with multi-gears. The rider would have to bend forward in order to reach the handlebars. The bike had complex gearing and complex braking. My guess is that the father selected a bike for her to grow into. As such, it was most likely too high up for her feet to touch the ground.

She tried to ride that bike but failed. Her father berated her and told her she was worthless. He said that she was bad because she didn't appreciate the money the bike had cost him.

For the next 30 years, she lived with those deep wounds and went on believing that she was indeed worthless and bad. That day at our bike camp she was utterly amazed that she could master bike riding in 30 minutes of stress-free fun. Throughout the process, she heard my comforting and reassuring words as I personally spotted her and launched her. For me, it was business as usual. The little I did that day was as easy for me as breathing. Getting her to master bike riding in 30 minutes was a piece of cake. I do it all the time and hardly give it a second thought.

After she regained her composure, the two ladies returned to the riding floor. She came up to me with an affectionate hug. She broke down, again in tears, and cried, "Why weren't *you* my father?"

I am conditioned to parents sobbing as they squeeze me, but I wasn't quite ready for this. This woman had not only been affected by the miracle of her daughter riding a bike; she too had experienced a miracle in her own sudden transformation. The torrents of pain and guilt that had been suppressed for her entire adult life erupted out of her. Up until that day, she hadn't recognized that she had been the victim of child abuse. She had accepted the labels of bad and worthless. That day, she was forced to deal with the realization that she had been carrying those scars for three decades—most of her life.

I will forever remember the impact our bike program had on her—and the impact she had on me.

The Morality Question

EARLY ON I EXPERIENCED a strange accusation. I was told by some that it was immoral to teach children with disabilities to ride bikes. The reasoning was that if the child acquired mobility, he or she would be exposed to the risk of getting injured or killed, such as in traffic.

My position is that the parent is the responsible party. The parent has the ability to take precautions such as locking up the bike so that it is inaccessible. I take the view that I will endeavor to teach any child if the responsible parent or guardian so requests.

The Bicycle Industry

BIKES HAVE BEEN AROUND since the mid-1800s. In today's era, bicycle manufacturing and sales are what I call a thin industry. Profit margins are small. The premier companies are largely focused on "top-down" marketing. The name brands sponsor race teams. Fans flock to buy the brand of winners in important races. Once the leading brand establishes a trend that consumers prefer, the discount store chains are usually quick in marketing look-alikes but with vastly inferior components and workmanship. I refer to these knock-offs as "disposable."

In the fabric of American culture, the usage of bikes, at least by adults, has become the pastime of the affluent. The bulk of retail bike shops are focused on satisfying that market. The economically disadvantaged often don't even own bikes. The few people in the lower economic strata who buy bikes tend to be happy with box store bargains that soon fail. A manifestation of this in American society is that the children of the lower class rarely have bikes. With less physical activity, there is a marked increase in obesity and related health issues for adolescents. Because the dominant activities for many children today are sedentary, the health and well-being issues of our children are profound and approaching epidemic proportions.

Virtually all bike dealerships are independent dealers. Independent is a fitting word to describe them. The owner and employees of a bike shop are there to support their addiction with bicycle culture and performance utilizing high-end bikes.

When I enter a bike shop I often get the feeling that the store employees resent my intrusion. I must not have the proper scars and the proper attire. The profit made in bike shops comes largely from two sources: sales of high-end racing bikes (costing thousands of dollars), and sales of supporting merchandise and accessories. The run-of-the-mill low-end bike isn't a money-maker. That's why so much of the typical shop's inventory is devoted to high-end performance bikes. The shop likes selling sophisticated bikes to informed customers who understand and appreciate such bikes. Both parties are pleased because it is a win-win. Cost is not a deal breaker. Bicycling aficionados tend to feel better the more they spend on their bikes and gear. In contrast, for low-end sales to uninformed customers, the bike shop salespeople and the customer both feel uncomfortable because neither will be happy. The last thing a bike shop wants is an unhappy customer going out the door, as the shop prides itself in being at the pinnacle of the biking culture.

The parent who enters a bike shop seeking a decent bike for a child with a disability has been left out of the marketing equation. Employees in a typical bike shop are clueless as to the needs of the challenged child. The segment of the market consisting of the parents of kids with special needs is miniscule and has been abandoned for all practical purposes.

The big box stores are yet another pitfall for parents of children with special needs. In addition to being poorly made, the bargain bikes are almost always made to appeal to the racing image. The combination of poor quality, absence of point-of-sale service, and an inappropriate design based on racing and competition seldom meets the needs of children with challenges.

Parents at our camps frequently drool over the bikes that I custom make, but my hand-crafted bikes are vastly more expensive to build than what the parent is willing or able to afford. My costs of production are roughly 10 times greater than the mass-produced bikes imported from Asia.

Here's a bicycle joke for you: "How do you make a small fortune in the bicycle business?" Answer: "You start with a large fortune."

It Doesn't Make My Heart Race

WHEN A PARENT BRINGS A BIKE TO ME for approval, it has usually been purchased from the box store. To be as kind and yet as truthful as possible, the expression I have developed is, "It doesn't make my heart race." Think this over: If the discount box store built airplanes, would you be willing to board that airplane on your next commercial flight?

In addition to the dreary cheapness of the box store bikes like BMX and freestyle, the bigger drawback is that those bikes simply aren't suitable for kids with disabilities. In the adaptive bike program, I custom build most of the bikes we use. I have developed a design that has stood the test of time. Bikes of my design have three features:

1. The crank is positioned at the mid-point between the front and rear tire contact points.
2. The crank position is then combined with a shorter crank arm. This means that the pedal, when in its highest position, is only about three-fourths of the height of the tire. For example, for 20-inch wheels, my pedal in its highest position does not exceed 15 inches. Because the pedal remains lower, as pedaling proceeds, the child's leg

position remains comfortable as the child rests on the saddle. For BMX and freestyle designs the pedal at its peak height is too high. The child can't pedal, remain seated, and also be able to reach the ground with a foot.

3. The front crossbar is no higher than the bike's wheel diameter.

There is hardly a box store bike out there that is designed this way.

The Analog Computer

PART OF WHAT I WAS ABLE TO ACCOMPLISH in the adaptive bike program was the result of my experience with analog computers.

Earlier in my career, my professional field of studies relied heavily on computers and simulation. Most readers have heard of digital computers; I also used an *electronic differential analyzer*, more commonly called an analog computer.

While digital computers are sequential devices and perform one operation at a time, the analog computer functioned as a simultaneous computing device. Voltages in various wires would change according to precise rules, and the voltages as an ensemble provided the desired outcome or solution to a problem. The computations were performed by electronic circuits and devices with a mass of wires going hither and yonder like spaghetti.

The DC voltages represented the variables, which were often displayed on a strip chart recorder. The analog computer had no screen and no keyboard. Instead it had other ways to measure and display voltages. In short, the analog computer could mimic the motion of physical devices, which included things like bicycles. When I wanted to alter a physical parameter, such as on the mathematical model of a bike, I had only to turn a knob, which changed the value of a variable resistance, referred to as a potentiometer.

Below is a patch panel of an analog computer.

How does this relate to the adaptive bike program? As I supervised children on bikes, in my mind I was merely tweaking potentiometer knobs because of my earlier training in the use of analog computers. I could change the outcome of their performance as if I were adjusting a knob, just like I adjusted the value of a parameter.

Three Omissions

THE ASTUTE READER will have noted by now three omissions in my story:

1. To date I have not given the program any catchy name or phrase. Certainly the adaptive bike program needs and deserves a name. Yes, the national charity iCan Shine, Inc. has adopted the name iCan Bike. Their adoption of a name is fine for them, but as a contract user of the equipment—of my design and manufacture—they will not give my intellectual property and program its name. Rainbow Trainers, Inc. is still in the process of evolving the program. I or my successors will give a name when the time is ready. Yet another motivation is the option of keeping that as an opportunity for future negotiations. A day will come when I as founder pass on to other pursuits. I have every confidence that the program will continue to evolve and grow. By not yet being named, some future benefactor, for example, might be enticed to come forward and in doing so place a name, possibly their name, on the program. This is called vanity, and it is

usually quite effective. In cases of philanthropy, the real benefactors are the children to be served.

2. My story stops somewhat abruptly *circa* 2019. Obviously the future will unfold, and it will be action-packed. My policy is to get to my destination, and only upon arrival will I announce to the world that I have arrived. I am still getting to my next destination.

3. My story is stingy with design details. I don't reveal the dimensions, tolerances, or a list of parts. I have intentionally kept the design details proprietary. I'm a capitalist, not a communist. Like the Little Red Hen, I have toiled for decades of my life. I stand firm in the belief that I am entitled to fair compensation for my efforts. Yes, others can look at a photograph or casually inspect one of my adaptive instruction bikes, but looking at what I have accomplished is vastly different from being able to replicate it. Moreover, I have priced my work so cheaply that any potential competitor would be well ahead of the game if they would merely contract with me for my services and/or intellectual ideas.

Into the Looking Glass

THE VISION OF THE ADAPTIVE BIKE PROGRAM came to me for many reasons. These reasons are very personal and unique to me. I apologize for sounding self-serving, but I have come to accept the fact that no other person in the world could have done this.

In order to accomplish any feat, three ingredients must come together:

1. Desire
2. Ability
3. Opportunity

I was born at the right moment in time, and the events of the world unfolded in a precise and necessary pattern to create the fertile ground. I can't even begin to list the circumstances or coincidences that happened to line up, almost like the planets, all in one unique sequence in time, a sequence that had a short period of existence.

The Banyan Tree

OF ALL THE TREES AND PLANTS that abound in God's world, I am most drawn to the banyan tree. The banyan tree starts off growing from a seed. It often grows in warm, tropical climates. Once the main trunk rises above the canopy of the surrounding vegetation, a strange thing happens. From the upper reaches of the banyan tree's foliage, a vine descends downward. At times the descending vine will make contact with the soil, where it will then send down roots. This vine then grows into a companion trunk that can support weight. This process repeats itself. Over time, the banyan tree has numerous trunks, which support an expansive canopy. I've seen a banyan tree in Fort Myers, Florida, at Thomas Edison's winter home, and I've seen another in Hawaii.

I feel a close association with the banyan tree, at least as a metaphor. Mathematics is my main trunk. With mathematics I was able to fight my way upwards, towards daylight. Once I had a clear view, I could drop a vine into some adjoining, and possibly confusing, situation.

Contrary to most people, I seek out confusion because I am the holder of certain unique tools that can bring order and light to displace chaos and darkness. In this manner I establish an additional trunk: expertise in a new area. The process then repeats. As a banyan tree, I have established myself as a respected and contributing problem-solver in a multitude of areas. I have substantial expertise in many areas, a multiplicity of trunks so to speak.

Perhaps I might even be described as a banyan tree on steroids. From my upper canopy vantage point, when I drop a vine I am venturing into some new fray. I'm careful as I make my plans to drop down a vine, and I try to select only the most ripe and confusing of targets. I drop that exploratory vine with considerable speed. Then, upon establishing ground contact, I sink roots by bringing myself up to speed with the local jargon and available literature. In today's world of Internet search engines, one can acquire knowledge and establish roots in a new domain with amazing quickness.

One trait of mine that often astonishes people is the speed with which I make decisions. That quickness occurs because of several quirks in my training and thought processes:

- Like the banyan tree, I look at things from above. When I see something that I like or that challenges me, I make my move swiftly.
- I accept my statistical chances. I don't require 100 percent of the information before making a move, but

rather I will make my thrust given only a possibility of being right. My thrust is primarily mental, so I am seldom committing monetary sums that I otherwise can't risk. When I come to a dead end, I accept my losses and retreat. Upon retreating, I wait like a hunter for my next target to come into view. I learned a long time ago that the prey will most likely be seen if the hunter is actively seeking it. Like all good hunters, I keep my eyes moving and constantly scanning.

- I make my moves boldly. I can later size up my hypothesis and either move forward or pull the plug and retreat.

- Over my lifetime, I have developed a sense of reliance on subroutines. The word "subroutine" comes from my training in FORTRAN programming. When a problem arises that is apt to come up again and again, you can use a program called a subroutine. You can author your own subroutine or borrow an existing subroutine from somebody else's library. The subroutine takes the required initial data and processes the information using a prepared logic structure. Upon arriving at a conclusion, the subroutine announces that it is done and sends back the answer to the main program.

- I believe strongly in exploiting *Pontryagin's Maximum (Minimum) Principle* [31]. In order to do anything in minimum time, the strategy is to apply full power (forward action) or full braking (reverse action). I have used two adjectives in naming the theorem: *maximum* and *minimum*. To a mathematician these are equal except for the polarity of the sign. The objective is to be at the extreme. Always be at the limits of your action possibilities, as that will cause your travel time to be at a minimum. People are often surprised when I abruptly reverse myself mid-stream, going from a full forward throttle position and then switching abruptly to a full backward. On the basis of this behavior, I have been described as being irrational. However, I consider myself to be perfectly rational. The outside observer is simply not aware of my algorithm for defining what is rational. Abrupt reversals in the conduct of one's affairs are entirely rational and consistent with attaining what are called time-optimal outcomes.

Through all of these things—like the numerous branches of the banyan tree—I was able to bring the adaptive bike program into being.

The Bike Logo

IF THERE IS ANY IMAGE that aptly represents the program, it is the Kleinian freehand sketch.

During my years of teaching at the University of Illinois, I often included bicycles in the lectures. On these days, I would start my lecture by doing a freehand sketch of a bike and rider on the chalkboard. That drawing became my trademark. I got to the point where I could do that sketch in two or three seconds.

I believe this simple sketch illustrates the joy of feeling the wind in one's face while riding a bicycle.

Lasting Effects

I AM AWARE that in my lifetime I have impacted many. After three decades of teaching at the University of Illinois my total student count came to about 5,000. From my perspective, the students fell into three categories.

One-third bitterly hated my guts. These were largely the memorizers, those who functioned in life by memorizing and then regurgitating facts but little else.

The middle third were the bumps on the log who just went along with the flow.

The final third consisted of those students who respected me and the wisdom that I tried to impart.

The memorizers felt threatened by me, so they tried to inflict harm on me by scurrying to the dean and the department head. Professionally, the petty complainers amounted to little. On the other hand, the ones craving my style of Socratic wisdom remained true, even to this very day. These are the ones who have become leaders and captains of industry.

Even given that great impact—5,000 students over three decades—it doesn't come close to that of the bike program. To date, we've worked with approximately 30,000 children, improving the lives of both the children and their families, and the potential for further impact is just beginning.

My Funding Sources

OVER THE YEARS, my research efforts were performed on a shoestring budget. I received no grants from the government. No company ever stepped forward to offer funding. I never solicited funding.

Because nobody ever funded the bicycle research, I could be as unbiased as possible and preserve my professional integrity. The funds, when required, typically came out of my own pocket, apart from a few relatively inconsequential exceptions.

T-Shirts

CERTAIN EXPRESSIONS reveal much about our society. Both bumper stickers and T-shirts can speak volumes. I will comment on some T-shirts slogans that have, or should have, appeared along the way.

I Understand. I speak with economy of language, so when I say "I understand" I have actually said five things:
1. I have heard you, and I understand what you said.
2. Now that I understand, I will start contemplating what you have said.
3. When and if it becomes appropriate, I will reply.
4. In the interim, this discussion is now concluded.
5. The floor is now open for us to move onto other matters.

I Am a Solution in Search of a Problem. The reflective reader will have figured out that, as a mathematician, I developed tools that allowed me to come up with solutions. Once I had a viable mix of solution methodologies at my disposal, I spent the bulk of my professional career searching for problems to which I could apply an available solution.

For example, my training as a systems theoretical mathematician introduced me to the stability concepts of A.M. Lyapunov (Russian mathematician, 1857-1918). Central to Lyapunov's work was the idea of *limit cycles*. A limit cycle will often manifest itself in certain classes of nonlinear differential equations. Limit cycles are self-generating, i.e. without external triggers or forcing functions. My approach to conducting research often centered on discovering some oddity where a system exhibited cyclical behavior for no obvious external reason. This is precisely what attracted me to the question of what causes glacial ice ages.

When I approached the glacial causation problem, I already had the solution. I merely had to verify that the misunderstood oscillations were caused by feedbacks and nonlinearities as Lyapunov had investigated. Hence, I became a solution in search of a problem.

My involvement with bicycles followed a similar pattern. The underlying mathematical mystery stemmed from the dynamics of an object or system with hinged joints. These systems are called *non-holonomic.* I understood how Cramer's rule, along with differential operators, can decouple such systems. From my training in feedback control principles, I recognized that the bicycle acted as a *non-minimum phase* system. A property of a non-minimum phase system is that it will exhibit counter-intuitive behavior. That explains why a bike goes in the opposite direction of a steering input.

In this book, I've cited three areas where I used the reverse approach of coming up with a solution and then identifying the problem: bicycles, tall buildings, and glacial causation.

I Am My Father's Son. It would be a mistake of some magnitude for a company to hire me to design widgets. The problem is that it is within my DNA to overbuild and over-specify. Over-specification in products is often costly. The company using my design services would suffer in the marketplace because few people want this level of quality. Instead they like cheap. Box stores specialize in and deliver cheap.

My father, Albert W. Klein (1910-1993), was a machinist and trouble-shooter for Bullard Machine Tool Company of Bridgeport, Connecticut. He would travel to factories throughout America and Canada, and fix broken Bullard machines. Bullard machines were usually massive in size and deeply complex.

Suppose the factory in a particular city depended on a critical Bullard machine to keep its assembly production line cranking out widgets. If production was halted due to a broken Bullard machine, my father's job was to get the ailing machine up and running. Pop always used overkill. If a bolt broke, he would typically drill additional holes and double or triple the number of bolts. The machine was back and running, though it may have looked ugly. What's more, it kept running.

I am my father's son. When I build adaptive instruction bikes or virtually anything else, they seldom fail.

This last T-shirt message is longer than many, but it is certainly a fact:

> Too bad the people
>> Who REALLY know
>>> How to run the country
>>>> Spend all their time
>>>>> Working on
>>>>>> Bicycles!

Christopher Columbus

I HAVE DEVELOPED a profound respect for Columbus and his approaches to problem solving. To me, the amazing thing about Columbus was not that he hit a land mass by sailing west but that he was able to get back home. After months of exploration, combined with thousands of miles of travel on uncharted seas, his navigation skills brought him within five miles of his desired return port of call. That port of call was one of the islands in the Azores, to the west of Portugal. He was able to sail directly to his desired destination because he knew its latitude. Each morning at dawn and each evening at dusk, Columbus used his sextant to measure the angle of the North Star above the horizon. Using this information, he merely had to make steering adjustments to maintain the proper latitude.

Upon arriving at that island's port, the town fathers accepted the claim that a new land lay to the west based on the evidence of Columbus's booty. Those town fathers were loyal to Portugal. Remember that Columbus, although Italian by birth, flew under the flag of Queen Isabella of Spain. The plan became clear. If Columbus and his ship and crew could be captured, then the

Portuguese would have exclusive knowledge of the land to the west and access to its riches.

However, upon reflection, the Portuguese officials had to abandon their plan to capture Columbus. Thirty or more of the local citizens had also seen the ship and the evidence of a new land to the west. A secret can never be a secret if 30 or more people have knowledge of it.

This story of Columbus applies to the adaptive bike program. Vast numbers of people have seen for themselves the program and how it can miraculously change children's lives. Even if I would suddenly vanish from the face of the earth and if all of the existing bikes and equipment were vanquished to some hidden world, the idea would still remain. Somebody at some point would go to the effort to recreate it.

A Third Question

I STARTED OFF THIS BOOK with two questions I am often asked:

- "How did you come up with the idea?"
- "Oh, did you do this because you have a child with a disability?"

There is a third question that typically comes from the more reflective observer, often a professional who works with children: "Gee, Dr. Klein, this program is amazing. Why didn't somebody come up with the idea before? What you are doing is so obvious. I can see the kids learn and evolve right in front of my eyes."

If this method of learning to ride a bike works so well, why didn't somebody come up with the idea before? Although unstated, I believe the person asking this question laments that they themselves didn't have the benefit of this training method as a child. Yet what we see is now obvious in hindsight but was not obvious in foresight.

I strongly hold the view that our entire culture believed one simple, yet enormous, lie: people with disabilities are incapable of riding a two-wheel bicycle. That's why so many people emphasized getting these kids onto contraptions with three and four wheels. I was able to envision that kids with wide variations in disabilities could indeed master two-wheelers. For me, this was a no-brainer as I recognized that the bike could be designed to be stable even without rider control. The notion of teaching kids with disabilities to ride bikes was simply never thought of before.

Throughout the history of science, engineering, and mathematics, keen minds always pursued truth and new frontiers. Both the Greeks and the Egyptians knew that the triangle consisting of 3, 4, and 5 formed a perfect right angle. Many sought a mathematical proof. Pythagoras solved the riddle.

The idea for vaccinating against various diseases came from a simple observation. A doctor in the British Isles noted that milkmaids tended to be immune from contracting smallpox. Investigation into this found that cows sometimes had a related disease called cowpox. When the milkmaids milked cows with cowpox, they sometimes had skin abrasions and cracks on their hands and fingers. After investigating this over a period of time, the doctors concluded that the exposure to cowpox in small doses caused the milkmaids to develop immunity to smallpox. This observation turned out to be the impetus to search for a smallpox vaccine, whereby humans could be injected with dead smallpox virus cells in order to develop immunity. Louis Pasteur is the one who finally made the big leap. He believed so strongly in the theory that he injected himself with his vaccine. Most skeptics assumed that Pasteur was a fool and that he would soon contract smallpox and die. Pasteur lived and was proved right. Again, we see that the advance happened because of the prior existence of something that created the vision.

When mankind observed birds flying, it was obvious that man could fly if only he had wings; thus, the idea of heavier-than-air flight was born. Though the Wright brothers were the first ones to build and fly a heavier-than-air machine, from the onset somebody was going to make that dream a reality. Others were actively pursuing the same goal at the same time, but it's estimated that the Wright brothers accelerated the attainment by a decade or more. My point is that the quest follows only after the goal is first envisioned.

In the case of the adaptive bike program, the idea of getting kids with disabilities on bikes was never a goal prior to my vision. I feel that my work stands out because I had the initial spark. Then I created an embodiment. Lastly, I brought the entire program into being. Therefore, my accomplishments fall into the category of landmark achievements. Once I had the vision, my work, like that of many others before me, boiled down to persistence along with the support of my wife. I am reminded of the quote attributed to Thomas Alva Edison: "Genius is one percent inspiration, and 99% perspiration."

I summarize the teaching of bike riding as follows:

- I have studied the rule book (actually, in my case I wrote the rule book).
- I am familiar with the basic moves.
- I come suited up ready to play.
- I come with the right equipment.
- I have played the game many times before.

Parting Words

IT IS MY SINCERE HOPE that you have enjoyed reading about how the adaptive bike program came into being.

A quotation attributed to Louis Pasteur seems appropriate: "Chance favors the prepared mind."

As for me, I'm quite comfortable giving God the credit for this program. This allows me to state very succinctly that the program came into being because God did it.

BICYCLES, FAITH, AND SPIRITUALITY

AT OUR BIKE CAMPS, I gave daily "sermonettes." I would deliver these five-minute talks during our lunch breaks, where I had a captive audience of staff, volunteers, and even parents.

My goal was to share some philosophy. For each of the five days of camp, I delivered a devotional related to better understanding bicycles, how children learn, or connections to theology. As a trained speaker, I was able to tailor my messages to reach even the most difficult of audiences—the teenage volunteers.

In this section, I provide selected sermonettes on The Theology of the Bicycle.

Fear Is All or Nothing

I FIND PARALLELS with bike riding and faith, including stability and balance in both a physical sense and a metaphorical one. When a bike and rider are zipping merrily along, they stay upright with relative ease, even though nothing visible is holding them up.

C. S. Lewis wrote in Perelandra (1944), page 68, "There is no reason why a man on a smooth road should lose his balance on a bicycle; but he could."

The point is that there is a certain mystery about a bike. We can't see anything holding the bike up, so it seems plausible that it might fall—unless we start to believe in the power of the invisible.

That is where faith and belief come into play.

I seldom discussed theology with learning children, but would occasionally do so when initiated by the child. In one such incident, a boy with Asperger's was at a camp in Wisconsin. Children with Asperger's tend to be highly intelligent. While riding on an adaptive trainer roller bike, the boy sang hymns and recited Scripture.

I couldn't match the boy's scriptural knowledge, but I did recite the passage in C. S. Lewis' Perelandra. The boy responded by asking, "Are you trying to say there's an analogy between riding a bicycle and our struggle in life with temptation and sin?" Impressed, I replied, "Yes."

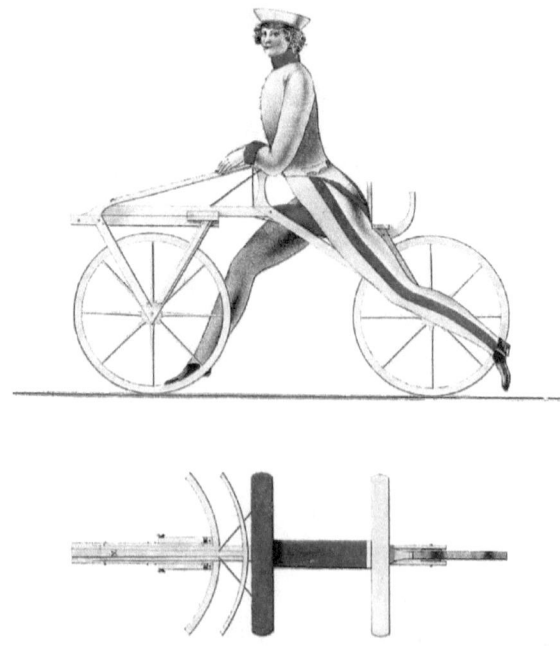

Upon looking in scriptural and biblical concordances for the word "bicycle," I find that somehow the biblical translators left that word out. Of course, bicycles didn't make their appearance until well after the writing of the Scriptures. The first verifiable claim for a bicycle is attributed to Baron Karl von Drais, a civil servant to the Grand Duke of Baden in Germany. Drais invented his Laufmaschine (German for "running machine") in 1817. Baron von Drais patented the design in 1818, which was the first commercially successful two-wheeled, steerable, human-propelled machine, then commonly called a velocipede.

Nonetheless, in the Bible we find analogies to the bicycle in terms of lessons to be learned. These lessons focus on balance, stability, and faith in the invisible.

Consider the distinctions between faith, hope, and belief. Vision is foundational to all three. One must have faith that a desired outcome will occur or is true. One has hope with regard to an outcome. One believes something is true, with less-than-perfect (i.e. unproven) knowledge.

In learning to ride a bicycle, one has to first have the vision—the notion that bikes are in the realm of possibility. If you believe you can ride, you are accepting an outcome on less-than-perfect knowledge. Hope implies that the outcome is out of one's control, but rather dictated by random chance. Faith implies that the outcome is largely determined by an external agent. In all cases, there must be some form of vision.

Bike riding is spiritual.

The human body is strange and sometimes counterintuitive. The brain is constantly firing, causing muscles to be tight. In order to relax, one has to condition the brain to stop sending out "contract" messages.

Fear, as a natural mechanism, causes tightness. The hands and arms become tight. The neck is stiff, the body is stiff. In contrast, skilled athletes can do much more than the average person because they've conditioned their bodies to do so. The athlete's muscles aren't tight.

We should strive to make our bodies and minds relax.

Upon relaxing, we are freed. Fear has been overcome. There is no such thing as half-fear—it is all or nothing.

Once we overcome fear, bike riding is as easy as riding a bike.

Look Forward, Not Down

WHEN RIDING A BIKE, the rider does not look down at their feet. Instead, the rider remains focused on what is ahead.

When we work with fearful, not-yet-riding children we often find that they are looking down at their feet, the front wheel of the bike, or the ground. In all my years of working with children, a child has never learned to ride a bike so long as they were looking down.

When a child is about to take that first ride, I try to entice them to relax, to look forward, or even to think about something else. I often say that in order to ride a bike, you need to do three things: pedal, keep looking forward, and smile.

Matthew 14: 26 – 31
When the disciples saw him walking on the lake, they were terrified. "It's a ghost," they said, and cried out in fear.
But Jesus immediately said to them: "Take courage! It is I. Don't be afraid."
"Lord, if it's you," Peter replied, "tell me to come to you on the water."

"Come," he said.
Then Peter got down out of the boat, walked on the water and
came toward Jesus. But when he saw the wind, he was afraid
and, beginning to sink, cried out, "Lord, save me."
Immediately Jesus reached out his hand and caught him. "You
of little faith," he said, "why did you doubt?"

When you are faced with danger and uncertainty, to look down and doubt is to assure that you will sink. If you want to follow Jesus, or if you want to merely ride a bike, you must look forward and believe. Looking down is a sucker's bet and will virtually always result in failure.

On the Back of Eagle's Wings

ONE RELEVANT PASSAGE is in Deuteronomy 32:10-11.

In a desert land he found him,
in a barren and howling waste.
He shielded him and cared for him;
He guarded him as the apple of his eye,
Like an eagle that stirs up its nest
And hovers over its young,
That spreads its wings to catch them
And carries them on its pinions.

Other translations suggest that the eagle stirs the nest, and in the process the young eaglets fall from the nest. The adult eagle has caused its young to fall from the nest, and yet carefully watches over them. If the young don't learn to fly in the process of falling, the adult eagle then swoops down and "carries them on the back of eagle's wings."

If you plan to transition a child to ride a bike, you should stir the nest. Get aggressive—by launching the child on a bike. Push the child off and simply let go. Of course, there is a skill required in knowing when to swoop down and catch the faltering child—on the back of eagle's wings.

In our adaptive bike camps we've worked with thousands of children so our swooping skills and timing are refined. If you hold onto the child or the bike, that child will not be able to learn on their own—to acquire wings of their own.

The Tuesday Question

AT THE END OF THE SECOND DAY of bike camp, typically a Tuesday, an anxious parent inevitably strikes up a conversation with me. The parent says something like this:

"Gee Dr. Klein, I've seen so much progress being made by all these children. Some kids are smiling, pedaling furiously, and almost ready to be riding. I can't believe it. (Note that the question of belief has been raised by the parent—or rather, the difficulty in believing.) I've noticed, however, that my son/daughter (fill in the name _____) isn't doing as well. Please tell me what we can do after the camp is over on Friday to help my child ride a bike."

Answering this parent's Tuesday question takes up valuable time that could otherwise be used to teach kids. When I run bike camps, I focus on the positive and spend my time getting kids to ride. I *don't* spend my time, especially early on in the camp, holding an anxious parent's hand and responding to a bunch of "what if's."

In short, I need a ready answer to this question, and here it is. I basically touch on a portion of the Sermon on the Mount, with focus on Matthew 6:34.

"So don't be anxious about tomorrow. God will take care of your tomorrow too. Live one day at a time." (The Living Bible)

All the worry in the world will not add one iota to your lifespan, it won't solve any problems, and it won't get a child to ride a bike any sooner. As our bike camps progress, I focus on teaching children to ride, not worrying about who won't ride and what I will do then. On the last day of each bike camp, typically Friday, the problems that were so central on Tuesday are either non-problems, as the child is now riding, or the problem is reasonably well-defined and is manageable using a number of standard techniques. These techniques, used only if needed, usually amount to prescribing a few procedures and equipment modifications so that the parent can complete the therapy.

Parents are always relieved and thankful when we finish the Tuesday conversation.

"Can I Buy a Bike?" and Other Faith Issues

ONE QUESTION I OFTEN GET from parents who are newly introduced to the therapy (where we use a roller bike) is "How do I buy a bike like that?" Indeed, even some professionals ask, "How might we buy one of these roller bikes?"

I am reminded of the story told in Mark 7:24-30. The story concerns a Syrian woman who approached the Master and besieged Him to cast a demon out of her daughter. The Master replied that His job was to help His own family (the Jews). The woman retorted, *"But even the puppies under the table are given some scraps from the children's plates."*

The Master replied, *"You have answered well…"*

The reality is that whether you can obtain an adaptive bike or not, you (the parent) have been given a far greater gift. And that gift is the gift of faith. For the first time in a long time, you now realize that your child is indeed capable of riding a bike. The years of doubt and bewilderment are now behind you. Your faith has made you free—because you believe that your child can be taught to ride a bike.

Of course you still want an appropriate bike, so now we have to build upon your faith. It isn't merely a matter of getting one bike, but rather an immersion in a process. The process starts with a few difficult steps, and you have now made those steps. You have faith, and you should now ask what to do next.

Already, your relationship with your child has changed, and for the better. You believe your child is capable of riding a bike. Your anxieties, doubts, and apprehensions are in remission. You are able to see your child as a bike rider, a child with a smiling face being fulfilled. Given that vision, the process of getting the child riding is relatively straightforward.

How Life and Theology Imitate Riding a Bike

THIS SERMONETTE follows my prior discussion about cats, dogs, and bike riding. With a bike and successful rider, *"each part in its own special way helps the other parts."*

It should come as little surprise that the same holds true for parts of the body of Christ. That's why we can say that "life and theology imitate riding a bike."

Of course, one could argue that riding a bike imitates life and theology, but I see it the opposite way—the bike comes first, and life and theology are imitations of bike riding.

Scripture tells us that the body of Christ—the church—is a single body composed of different parts, the individual members. Consider Romans 12:4-5:

> *"Just as there are many parts to our bodies, so it is with Christ's body. We are all parts of it, and it takes every one of us to make it complete, for we each have different work to do. So we belong to each other, and each needs all the others."*

Becoming a successful bike rider requires the rider to act in a fluid manner, becoming one with the bike. The meaning is clear:

Each part in its own special way helps the other parts.

The One-Track Mindset

IN OUR CONTEMPORARY SOCIETY, it seems we have developed a stigma against people or things that are "one-track." Popular wisdom suggests we are always better off if we have an open mind, and support from many viewpoints. People with one-track minds are thought of as almost irrational or dominated by tunnel-vision.

If we extend this thinking to bicycles, we raise the question as to whether it's safer to have two wheels or three wheels. Let's consider the question: Is it better to ride bicycles or tricycles?

My position is that bicycles are vastly superior to tricycles. Bicycles are "single-track" vehicles, whereas tricycles are multi-track. I contend that except in the most extreme cases, single-track vehicles are best, and even safer than multi-track vehicles.

An interesting reversal occurs with bicycles and tricycles. A stationary two-wheeled bike will fall over, but a two-wheeler in motion can acquire dynamic stability where the bike remains upright of its own accord due to speed. Conversely, a stationary tricycle will remain quite upright, but when motion is added (especially when speed is combined with adverse conditions), the tricycle is easily upset and is prone to throwing the rider for a spill.

When faced with a bumpy road or the need to make a sharp turn, a tricycle rider experiences a sudden loss of stability. Without warning, one wheel (a support point) will become airborne. The trike has suddenly become a two-wheeler, and the rider is unprepared. He will usually get thrown from the tricycle and will often get injured.

Yes, I am saying that tricycles, when operated at speeds comparable to bicycles, are considerably more hazardous than their bicycle counterparts.

Tricycles are poor dynamic vehicles precisely because they are multi-tracked. When an outside wheel of a tricycle hits a bump or hole, the wheel is lifted or dropped, and more significantly, the vehicle is tossed and rolled. Rolling results from hitting a bump off center because the wheel being struck is off-center. The rider had little or no advance warning of the upsetting action and has never been conditioned to develop corrective feedbacks.

Bicycles as single-track vehicles, however, are amazingly robust and are relatively impervious to external disturbances. Hitting a bump or a pothole may not be much fun, but the bike will tend to remain upright as the bump causes a sudden impact that's in line with the frame and the mass of the bike and rider. The rider may experience a jolt, but the jolt is usually in the head-on direction, and the bike makes it past the disturbance. Some bike riders actually enjoy hitting bumps and riding over rough terrain. The sales of mountain and all-terrain bikes reflect this pursuit of sport. Of course the bike industry has invented clever suspension systems to ease the shock of the bumps. The bumps provide an exciting ride, but ultimately bikes are immune to being upset, especially when rider skill is added, using the legs as shock absorbers.

There are times in life when the wise decision is to be of a one-track mind. Be sure of the firmness of your belief, and then place your trust in that belief. John 14:6 tells us:

Jesus answered, "I am the way and the truth and the life. No one comes to the Father except through me. If you really knew me, you would know my Father as well. From now on, you do know him and have seen him."

Those who believe it's better to have multiple supports in place, such as belief in theory X, religion Y, diet Z, make-over Q, or whatever it is that turns them on, are more apt to be upset when an obstacle is encountered or when one of their pillars gives way. In contrast, if you have the right kind of bike, or if you are armed with faith built on a rock, you are on a single track vehicle, but it's the correct vehicle.

Those Nasty Bushes and Pavement Cracks

AS WE JOURNEY THROUGH LIFE, we are constantly at risk. Temptations tug at us. The evil one constantly lurks in the shadows.

A friend of mine told me the story of his mother, who lived in Hungary prior to World War II. She had never ridden a bike as a child, but did learn as an adult, at age 40. My friend commented that the bike, when ridden by his mother, had a magnetic attraction to bushes and obstacles. As she rode her bike on a trail and came near a bush, she would invariably end up crashing into it.

The reason is clear: She was focusing on the bush and not on the road ahead of her. By focusing on the bush, her motor reflexes, driven by fear, subconsciously caused her arms to steer away from the bush. The problem is that the act of turning away, even subconsciously, caused her steering action to shift the bike's ground contact point away from the bush, with the result that the bike was now leaning *toward* the bush. Bikes tend to go in the direction of lean, because this is the only way to restore balance. Moreover, the tendency of a front fork to turn into the direction of lean is an intentional attribute of the shape of the front fork.

When a bush or other hazard in life menaces you, the best approach is to look beyond. Plan your actions to keep you on that course.

Another serious hazard in riding a bicycle arises when the front wheel falls into a crack in the road surface. This is especially a risk factor for road cyclists, as the tires of modern road bicycles are very narrow and the rider may be riding too fast to spot the crack in time. When the front tire falls into a crack, the front fork is now unable to turn, and therefore the rider is unable to apply steering corrections. A sudden and violent crash often results.

A deep biblical question that has faced theologians for a seeming eternity is whether man has free will or whether his fate is predestined, ordained by God. I, for one, am of the view that these two positions are not contradictory but rather compatible. Ephesians 1:4-11 tells us:

> "For he chose us in him before the creation of the world to be holy and blameless in his sight. In love he predestined us for adoption to sonship through Jesus Christ, in accordance with his pleasure and will—to the praise of his glorious grace, which he has freely given us in the One he loves. In him we have redemption through his blood, the forgiveness of sins, in accordance with the riches of God's grace that he lavished on us. With all wisdom and understanding, he made known to us the mystery of his will according to his good pleasure, which he purposed in Christ, to be put into effect when the times reach their fulfillment—to bring unity to all things in heaven and on earth under Christ. In him we were also chosen, having been predestined according to the plan of him who works out everything in conformity with the purpose of his will."

The essence is that when we ride a bike, we have the freedom to apply torques onto the handlebars either logically or willy-nilly.

When a child is placed on a bike for the very first time, experience tells us that the steering actions are apt to be wrong—to the point that the child crashes. Experience also tells us that the mature rider who has the misfortune of getting the front wheel stuck in a crack can't steer and also crashes. In contrast, when a child does master bike riding, the steering actions are the child's free will, but they are also compatible with what it takes to stay upright and to navigate wherever the child wishes to go.

A favorite hymn has the words that sum up these thoughts: "We are given the freedom to do what is not pleasing to God; until the Holy Spirit changes our will to be God's will."

Let Kids Be Kids

A COMMON BELIEF in American society today is that our kids are somehow substandard in math and science. We are frequently told that children in other countries, Asian countries in particular, are outperforming American children in these critical areas. The presumption is that we are in the midst of a national downfall, and urgent corrective action is needed. The usual prescription is to lengthen the school day and calendar, start kids in school at earlier ages, spend more time on drill, cram in more academics, and continually push our kids as we strive to emulate the Asian culture. The "Tiger Mothers," to quote a newly coined phrase, are often at the forefront of those pushing for more and more.

I strongly believe that the primary task of childhood is childhood. Simply stated, we need to let kids be kids. When left to their own devices, kids take play very seriously. Their imagination is sparked. Every act and thought is directed at achieving their ultimate goal. Through play, children engage their minds and bodies to emulate adults—at least as they view adults.

It's important to distinguish what is meant by "play." I'm not referring to adult-directed activities such as team sports, spelling bees, or piano lessons. Instead I'm thinking of whatever kids do when they are left to their kid-directed imaginations. Tiger Mothers stress memorization and subsequent regurgitation of adult-defined facts at adult-defined performance standards. This Tiger Mother mania is predicated on the myopic premise that fact-level knowledge and pseudo adult emulation are paramount, oblivious to the realization that knowledge and facts are relatively minor precursors to higher levels of creativity—let me even utter the word "genius."

Genius is a wonderful thing. Likewise, creativity is a wonderful thing. Genius and creativity self-ignite within a person. They aren't things that an adult can teach. The best adults can strive for is to foster a setting that allows genius and creativity to spring forth from within the child. Children who are allowed the freedom to truly play are forever pushing their imaginations. Said another way, children need to be allowed to color outside of the lines.

As an illustration of the problem, across many levels in academia, courses are designed to prepare the student for the next class in so-and-so topic. Even at the university level, where I taught for three decades, I was amazed at how many courses and textbooks have titles such as "Introduction to..." Then, once the student takes the next course, its stated goal is—you guessed it—to prepare the student for yet another loftier course. At some point academia needs to get real and start redirecting classes so that students who finish a course will exit with skills that make them functional in the marketplace.

Children are not merely adults in training. Children are people with distinct powers and joys. A happy childhood is measured by the children themselves, and is based on their own perception of themselves.

What are the blessings of childhood? The first is that children enjoy the gift of moral innocence. The second is the gift of openness to the future. Children are free to imagine whatever might come into their minds. Adults, in contrast, become restricted by their obsession with their own plans and expectations for a defined future. Children alone are free to imagine the most improbable of adventures. A third blessing of childhood is that time is plentiful. Time drags on so slowly in our growing years that it is impossible to waste. Anxious adults, on the other hand, are deluded into thinking that time can somehow be wasted. For kids forced to endure some adult-directed activity—I'll use school as an example—time is the enemy as the hands of the clock seem to be glued in place. Time virtually stops when having to listen to a stuffy teacher expounding on some endlessly boring topic such as sentence diagramming, conjugating Latin verbs, or memorizing absurd lines from Shakespeare's *The Merchant of Venice*. In my opinion, the real adventures in life can only start when the afternoon school bell rings, signaling the moment of release from an adult-imposed prison.

Jesus frequently praised children and welcomed their company. Jesus even commanded adults to emulate children,

"… unless you become like a little child, you shall not enter the kingdom of God." Matthew 18:3

Many parents today would benefit by taking a reflective time-out from teaching our children dull, adult-directed dribble to discover how much we can learn from children. A second assignment for parents would be to take the time to ride a bike— and I mean *really* ride a bike. For example, try riding a bike with no hands. Once that is achieved, see if you have the courage to ride a bike with four people on board.

Bikes are social. Bikes are spiritual. Bikes allow us the time to reflect on the physics and mathematics of the world. Bikes reinforce decision-making skills as the decisions must come increasingly quicker as the rider's speed increases. Bikes allow us to believe in ourselves, to do something perfectly, and to have faith in

God's promises.

Note: Some of the ideas above are taken from *The Wall Street Journal*, Opinion Page, February 9, 2011, article by James Bernard Murphy, "In Defense of Being a Kid."

The Perfect Rider

OVER MY YEARS OF WORKING WITH CHILDREN, I have always adhered to certain protocols. Because some children were apprehensive about this big, lurking stranger, I developed a bedside manner that helped them relax. I started off by asking the child's age, often suggesting an exaggerated age, such as 13 when I sensed that the child was perhaps 10. I made a modest deal of being wrong, asking again with a surprised look if they weren't really older. Once I was corrected by the child and properly humbled, I proceeded to make a few more inquiries. My technique was to ask questions they were able to answer without much difficulty. I asked if they had brothers and sisters. I asked their favorite color. If I suspected the child was already a bike rider, I asked if the child was able to ride a bike. If they answered, "Yes," I asked the next question, "Are you any good (at riding a bike)?"

The amazing thing was that in virtually every case the child smiled and replied with a strong, "Yes." I have no recollection of any child who was a bike rider ever telling me that they *weren't* good. When we think about it, is there any child who can ride a bike who also feels that he or she isn't good at it? If so, I've never encountered one.

But when instructing children, especially those with disabilities, the parents may have a different view. This is especially true if the parent is big into biking. I have noted that parents who are into biking tend to be critical of other riders, especially beginning and struggling riders. These self-styled experts often question the fit of the child on the bike. In the adaptive bike program, we keep the seats sufficiently low so that the child is able to place their feet flat on the ground while seated on the saddle. Of course, this means the leg won't fully extend. The ostensible experts don't miss the opportunity to point this out. A second commonly voiced concern, especially for children with cerebral palsy, is that the child's feet don't maintain proper placement on the pedals. In many cases their feet will be pointed outward, and sometimes the child's foot is placed with the pedal under the heel, as opposed to the arch or ball of the foot.

My response is to politely acknowledge and then dismiss these comments. I thank the parents for their concern but remind them that the child is in the process of learning to ride a bike, and that learning to ride is easier if the child can place their feet on the ground. I reassure the parents that proper leg extension will come but only after the child has mastered other critical aspects, notably balancing while pedaling.

Improper fit on a bike, if there is such a thing, has never been a reason to prevent a child from becoming a bike rider. A classic illustration of this is the child diagnosed with mild hemiplegic conditions. My observation is that a person with one strong and properly functioning side of the body, usually described as hemiplegic, can still become a remarkably capable bike rider. The bicycle and rider, once in motion, have an incredible capacity to achieve perfection. Perfection comes as the bike and rider appear to glide along smoothly, almost like a bird in flight. The rider pedals with amazing ease and experiences the joy of the "wind in the face."

"I tell you the truth, whoever hears my word and believes him who sent me has eternal life and will not be condemned; he has crossed over from death to life." John 5:24

My observation is that when a person accepts the grace offered by Christ, we aren't told that the rider lacks proper leg extension or has improper foot placement. Salvation through acceptance of God's grace is a holistic step. There is no graduation or degree of salvation, just as there is no such thing as an imperfect bike rider.

Suffering, Endurance, Character, and Hope

WHEN A CHILD experiences failure in attempting to ride a bike, the child feels defeated. This defeat is often accompanied by a jolt and even pain. As a result, the child may adopt a negative attitude. An all too common outcome is the "I hate biking" mindset. To place a child with this attitude on a bike is the epitome of suffering.

Humans typically follow the most basic of instincts: to fight or to flee. The trick is to stand and fight—to accept suffering. Romans 5:3-4 is instructive:

> *"Not only so, but we also glory in our sufferings, because we know that suffering produces perseverance; perseverance, character; and character, hope."*

Suffering leads to endurance. Endurance builds character—the character to persevere. With character comes hope.

The hope is merely that mastery of whatever will come. The child who desires bike mastery will follow the progression as stated by Paul in his letter to the Romans.

Gymnasiums and Other Gods

IT'S INTERESTING TO PONDER why schools have physical education and sport programs. My naïve view is that physical education, especially in elementary schools, should provide exactly that: education to children. The goal should be for the children to become more physically fit. Unfortunately, that is not always the case.

One premise, though seldom expressed, is that the human mind will function better if the body is fit, and so we strive in education to nurture both the mind and the body. Another premise is that as we grow, especially in our early formative years, we can benefit from help in proper development of our motor abilities, just as we can benefit when receiving help in developing higher thought processes.

Human movement is complex due to the preponderance of joints, muscles, tendons, vision, body feedback, and the body's controlling brain and nervous system. It's a fallacy to think that all humans will somehow automatically optimize the organization of their bodies and develop good coordination.

As humans grow, we learn to perform simple tasks, first as

infants and then as older children. Typical tasks include reaching to grasp an object, throwing a ball, walking upright on both legs, hopping, swimming, and riding a bicycle. Of course, not all people are equally gifted. Some people seem to have natural agility.

Even excellent athletes strive to become better, as they often seek coaching at all levels. For example, major league baseball pitchers are photographed in motion using cameras that transmit images to computers for subsequent analysis. The objective is to identify inefficiency in the movements so as to bring about a greater level of performance. As a general rule, the improvement is based on improving the efficiency of the entire human body, thus increasing the use of more simultaneous degrees of freedom.

When I reflect on my adolescent years in the 1940s while attending Wilcoxson Grade School in Stratford, Connecticut, I recall that we had recess, but nothing I would call physical education. During recess, if it wasn't cold or raining, the class would go outside onto the playground for our appointed fifteen or so minutes. We would often pick teams and play a competitive game, like softball or dodgeball. Other times we would be free to spend our time as we wished, playing jump rope, shooting baskets, shooting marbles, or standing around talking.

In today's jargon, it would be fair to say I was a clumsy kid. I was tall and lanky and had poor coordination. I was never selected to be pitcher of the team, or first baseman, or shortstop, but rather relegated to some outfield position, typically right field. When teams were picked, I was usually among the last to be selected, along with one or two other really uncoordinated kids. When in right field I dreaded the idea that somebody would hit the ball towards me because I feared I would mess up and not catch the ball.

I can recall going out for the football team in high school. At the end of the first drill, the coach had all the new kids line up at one end of the practice field and we then raced to the other end.

Obviously, the coach wanted to know who his best runners were. It wasn't me. I wasn't best; I was last out of 70 or so would-be ninth-grade football players.

As I reflect back on sports, physical education, and motor movement, I now realize that one reason I was a slow runner was that nobody ever taught me how to run. I say "taught me how to run" because running involves developing and executing a motor plan. Although I've never sought the advice of an expert, my hunch is that I was a poor runner because I didn't use all of my parts, or at least not properly. In particular, I suspect that I ran mostly with my legs and thighs, but I lacked the "spring" of using my ankles to spring me forward with each stride.

As we perform simple movements, we develop patterns of habitual muscle actions, and some of us don't optimize as well as others. That's why some people have a natural gift for athletics, and others are, let's say, clumsy.

One of my favorite movies is "Max Dugan Returns," script by Neil Simon (1983). In particular I like the scene where the young boy Michael McPhee (the film debut of Matthew Broderick) is doing poorly in Little League. As he walks away dejected after striking out, an older man, a stranger to him, approaches. It turns out the stranger is Charley Lau, the batting coach of the Kansas City Royals, hired by the eccentric grandfather (Jason Robards) to teach the boy how to hit. When introducing himself to the discouraged boy, the coach says things like, "Kid, you are lousy. But it's not your fault. Nobody ever taught you how to hit."

Of course the boy does learn how to hit well when coached, and wins the final game of the season and all that.

In my opinion, physical education should be about spotting and working with developing children to allow them to be better athletes and have better motor coordination. Another aspect of game playing is sportsmanship—something that's in short supply in our society. With improved motor skills and physical fitness come improvements in self-esteem, ability to interact socially, increased speed in processing images as the world moves, as well as a host of other attributes including the smile factor.

Other than my brief try at freshman football, I never went out for any team sport. Competitive sports were not fun for me, and I only participated to the extent that I was required to by adults, or when the whole neighborhood gang of kids decided to play a ball game.

In all my years of education, from kindergarten to college, I have no recollection of any physical education teacher actually teaching "physical education." Instead, we would scrimmage for most of the period and then run a few laps. We were never coached. Our high school PE teacher had been in that position since my father attended high school. After three decades of being the PE teacher, he had reduced his level of involvement to that of assembling the kids, checking off names, tossing out a ball, blowing a whistle, and retiring to the teachers' lounge.

Varsity sports are predominantly about winning. With winning comes ego-building and building a financially solid, self-sustaining sports program. By the time we're in top-tier colleges and universities, winning and dollars are paramount. Athletic directors of major schools are in the business of attracting and recruiting star athletes and then keeping the coffers filled with cash from donors.

"Then he entered the temple area and began driving out those who were selling. 'It is written,' he said to them, 'My house will be a house of prayer, but you have made it a den of robbers.'" – Luke 19:45-46

Institutions of education that have constructed sports facilities under the guise of physical education, and yet who manage these facilities for the purpose of glorification of winning sports teams are way off the mark when it comes to serving the physical education needs of the students. In selecting locations for our adaptive bike program, where I assert that physical education is the goal, we can't overturn the tables of the money changers in the temple, but we can take our program elsewhere. If athletic directors and coaches object to permitting adapted activities within their sacred shrines, we know we're in the wrong place.

Please note that I have no objection to competitive sports per se, but I do strongly object to operating under the guise of physical education when that is inherently not the case.

A Ram in the Bush

IN THE SUMMER OF 2015, I met a minister in Richmond, Virginia. She made a point of describing the adaptive bike program as "a ram in the bush."

When Abraham went to give a sacrifice to God, he had only his son Isaac to offer. Just as Abraham was prepared to sacrifice Isaac, a ram appeared and was caught in a bush. Abraham was able to sacrifice the ram in place of Isaac. God will provide.

The bike program is a ram in the bush because it is a way that God provides for His children, including children with disabilities who, prior to our program, had few alternatives.

Prepare Ye the Way

WHEN RIDING ON A SMOOTH PATH, it's easy to take it for granted.

My wife, Marjorie, recalls her childhood on her parents' farm in rural Iowa. Bike riding was difficult on roads of loose gravel or on grassy lawns and pastures. Avoiding the occasional "cow-pie" was also a concern. Obviously, it's harder to pedal and balance on a bicycle in such conditions. Marjorie's choice of transportation, whether for fun or for getting around, was usually her pony as opposed to a bicycle.

In developing countries, roads and paved surfaces are not always available. If the way has not been prepared, it's difficult to ride a bike. Instead the means of transportation might be horse, camel, or even just walking.

There's little wonder that water played such a historical role in travel, as ships could carry cargo and passengers down a river, along a coastline, or over open seas from country to country. Even if the waterway was narrow or hazardous, it provided a path of least resistance. It would often be easier to walk along the stream, say, as opposed to climbing over rugged terrain.

Isaiah spoke prophetic words as he told the ancient biblical people,

"A voice of one calling: prepare a way for the Lord; make straight in the wilderness a highway for our God." Isaiah 40:3

To "prepare" meant to remove all obstacles and obstructions. In the days of Isaiah, if an important person were to come, such as a king from a neighboring kingdom, then the roads would be leveled and made safe.

Isaiah was saying, in effect, to make a highway through the wilderness by which God would lead the people of Judah back to resettle their land. Through the prophet Isaiah, God spoke:

"Every valley shall be raised up, every mountain and hill made low; the rough ground shall become level, the rugged places a plain." Isaiah 40:4

As a metaphor, this imagery points to the need for an ethical and spiritual preparation for the Lord's coming.

Malachi 3:1 echoed the Isaiah passage by noting that the messenger of the Lord *"will prepare the way before"* him. Luke 1:17 appears to refer to the Malachi passage and the coming of the Messiah by also calling for an ethical and religious reformation as the way to prepare. In those biblical days, it was the custom for a country to call for ethical reform to prepare a people for the Lord. God had even more in mind when He spoke of "every valley" being "raised up" and "every mountain and hill" being "made low." This highway imagery appears in Isaiah 35:8 and elsewhere in the Bible. Isaiah was able to see a future time when the Lord Himself would appear.

The simple act of riding a bike is analogous to being a special person for whom the way has been prepared. When a child is empowered to ride a bike—on the prepared path—the child is then able to glimpse the power and glory of the Lord.

APPENDIX A: A How-To Primer for Parents

LEARNING TO RIDE A BIKE is a significant milestone. Some children pick it up easily while others get too discouraged or scared after a few falls to even continue. Whether your child has never tried to ride a bike or has tried and not done so well, this step-by-step guide can help.

Getting Back in the Saddle

Before getting to my step-by-step guide, I'd like to offer some hope to those who have tried to help a child ride a bike, but after one or more failed bike riding attempts, just can't get the child to try again.

As you may have noticed with your own child, kids who are unsuccessful in learning to ride tend to go through three distinct phases where they become increasingly hostile to bike riding:

"I can't ride a bike."
This initial phase becomes rooted in the child's mind after several failed attempts at riding, usually ones that end in falls and bruises.

"I don't like riding a bike."
This second phase is where we start to see signs of hostility toward bike riding.

"I hate biking!"
In this third phase, the child adopts a total hatred of riding a

bike. Now getting that child to become a bike rider is a monumental task.

I have made it my life's work to get these hard-core, bike-hating kids onto bikes, and they become completely transformed in the process. The national adaptive bike program, *iCanBike*, was patterned after my brainchild. Unique bikes of my design, along with specialized instructional techniques, have been adopted throughout North America to serve children with disabilities. The program has helped tens of thousands of children, making it the largest and most successful program of its kind. And what's great is that the knowledge and techniques of the program can be applied to *all* children.

8 Steps to Success

Bike riding is a skill the child learns by *doing* as opposed to being *taught*. The best thing you can do is set your child up for success and then get out of their way.

Here are 8 easy steps to get your child on the road to bicycle mastery:

Step 1: Choose the right bike.

Get a bike that the child will feel comfortable on. I suggest a cruiser style, as opposed to a thin-tired racing bike. The cruiser is actually a throwback to bikes of the 1950s and 1960s with big balloon tires, comfortable triangular seat, single speed, coaster brake (applied when pedaling backwards), and handlebars that come up fairly high. There should also be a brake on the rear tire, operated by a lever on the right handlebar.

Beginner bikes should have these five basic design principles:

1. The pedal height at the top of the arc is no higher than 75% of the wheels' diameter.
2. The crank is positioned mid-way between the two wheels (many cranks are too far back).

3. The crossbar is no higher than the top of the wheel.
4. The seat has a proper and comfortable fit for the child.
5. The handlebars are raised about five inches over what would otherwise be common.

Example of a proper learning bicycle

Example of an inappropriate learning bicycle

Step 2: Adjust the bike for learning.

Lower the seat so that the child can easily reach the ground with both feet while seated on the bike. Then raise the handlebars so that the child is looking forward (as opposed to looking down at the ground or feet) when holding the handlebars. I recommend using a stem riser to raise the handlebars. Lastly, remove both of the pedals.

Step 3: Provide a suitable environment for learning.

Now, find a wide, open, flat area, such as a vacant parking lot. Avoid hazards such as curbs, trees, storm drains, a narrow sidewalk, traffic, etc. Remove as many distractions as possible, including well-intended but overly exuberant siblings or family members, neighbors, pets, and friends. Though it's tempting to use a grassy lawn to soften the falls, this makes it harder for the child to get up to speed since the softer surface makes it harder to pedal. Instead opt for a paved surface and a trusty spotter to swoop in for a save when necessary.

Do anything else necessary to ensure the child is in peak condition: well-fed, hydrated, dressed in comfortable weather-appropriate clothing (cool weather is preferable so they can wear long-sleeves and pants for added protection; elbow and knee pads are good too).

Step 4: Prepare to be a spotter.

The spotter needs to do two things:

Don't interfere. You must allow the child to discover how to ride a bike, even if the rider and bike are wobbly and look like they are about to fall. The learning rider hesitates and has delayed reactions, which is why they appear wobbly. Too much intervention suffocates the natural discovery, which leads to the child becoming increasingly stiff and less confident, which leads to the spotter being increasingly compelled to intervene.

When I ask those trapped in this self-defeating scenario why they don't simply let go, they say, "I have to hold on or else the child will fall." In truth, the child is more apt to fall because they haven't yet had the opportunity to experiment and discover that the bike can be easily balanced merely by steering into the fall.

Also, explaining too much to the child hurts more than it helps.

I was once invited to teach biking skills at a school for the deaf in North Carolina. The teachers used only the simplest of signs and gestures to communicate. I was amazed at how quickly bike learning can happen when nobody is uttering a single word. Whenever the spotter is talking, the child becomes fixated on processing the words from the spotter instead of listening to what the bike is telling them. Let the bicycle talk to the child.

Come to the rescue. The best approach is to allow the child to attempt riding and possibly even fail at times. The spotter should be positioned, able, and prepared to swoop in and save the child from the inevitable fall. The person spotting must know when a bicycle's seemingly precarious wobble is normal and a natural part of the learning process, and when the converse is true. In general terms, a little wobble is okay and a big wobble means it's time to swoop in.

Spotting requires considerable running, agility, and endurance. It also requires alertness and quickness of hands should a save become necessary. If you aren't up to the task, find a friend, relative, or neighbor who can run and who has fast hands. Whoever ends up spotting, be sure to run quickly alongside the child after launch (close enough to grab the bike if needed but far enough to offer the child space to learn; about 2 feet), and be prepared to grab the handlebars and seat simultaneously to save the child from falling.

Step 5: Launch (and run fast)!

Have the child put on his/her helmet. Hold the bike steady and upright (not leaning to either side) while the child gets on. The child should be straddling the bike with both feet touching the ground.

Then… launch the child swiftly! Going slowly makes it harder for the child to achieve balance as bikes become more stable with speed.

Run alongside the child with your hand on the back of the

seat, then release your grip once the bike is launched. This way the child can discover how to ride without the bike's tip and motion being altered by the spotter's hand holding onto the bike.

Encourage the child to coast a little between pushes. Instruct them that if they start to fall, they should apply the hand brake to stop and put their feet down. Tell them, "You will not fall, and you will not hurt yourself if you use the brake and put your feet down."

The trick to riding a bike is to turn the handlebars gently in the direction that the bike starts to fall. In steering into the fall direction, the child will amazingly discover that the bike steadies itself. Once the child can go, say, 20 feet with a good push, then it's possible to maintain balance by just steering. The child should not use their body to shift side to side; they should always turn the handlebars towards the direction of fall.

Step 6: Move to a slight incline.

Once the child feels comfortable on a flat surface, try launching on a slight downgrade. The child should use a "frog push" where the child swings both feet forward at the same time, then pushes back with both at the same time. If they get going too fast, they can use the hand brake.

Step 7: Put the pedals back on.

Put the pedals back on the bike and repeat the steps above. The child should initially use the pedals only as footrests. Again, if they begin to fall, they should use the hand brake to stop and put their feet down.

Once the child can go 50 to 100 feet on a down slope with feet on pedals, then try again with a gentle pedaling action.

Step 8: Smile!

Encourage the child to relax and smile. Have them sing a song as they ride. Far too many learning riders are stiff because they are afraid. Stiffness makes it harder to ride a bike, so try to get them to relax and enjoy it. If they get tired or scared, stop. Have fun. Don't overdo it, but work on it gradually.

Off and Away!

Remember that the child discovers how to ride a bike. It is an ah-ha moment, and once it occurs, two things are true:

- It's as easy as riding a bike.
- Once you learn, you never forget.

Think about passengers on commercial airlines. Simply riding in a plane doesn't qualify a person to fly one. To become proficient as a pilot, one must sit at the controls and actively manipulate them. The same can be said for bike riding. As long as the spotter is holding onto the bike and keeping it upright, the rider is just a passenger. Until the child can control the bike's movements on their own, they can't really learn what to do.

Launch and let go!

It usually only takes a few tries—and a few minutes—for everything to "click" with the child, as long as all the steps above have been followed properly. Sure, sometimes a child can succeed even without following these steps, but by following this guide you are more likely to get your child riding quickly and without many bruises.

The ah-ha moment usually comes suddenly and unexpectedly but most often once the proper conditions have been put into place. As mentors, our role is to set the stage for the discovery to occur. With this how-to primer for parents, it is my fervent wish that you and your child will indeed achieve every success.

Blessings and Happy Pedaling,
Richard E. Klein

APPENDIX B: Bicycle Physics 101

THIS APPENDIX delves into the physics of how and why wide tires and rollers cause a bicycle to be more benign, making discovery of balancing easier. I will start by addressing two opposing but related topics: why bicycles fall over and why bicycles don't fall over.

A stationary or improperly steered bicycle falls over because it is top-heavy. The center of gravity is above or on top of the support point. Any imbalance causes the center of gravity to fall. Said in a joking sense, a bicycle falls over because it is too tired.

When a bicycle of proper design with proper steering is moving forward, the bike and rider rarely fall. The bike and rider tend to remain upright because of steering actions. The steering causes the wheel contact points to be constantly moving or shifting laterally, as viewed from the rider's perspective. The combination of forward movement and continual, proper steering achieves the desired balance. Bicycles by design act to self-steer. The precession of the spinning front wheel aids in correct steering. Also, the front fork's shape helps, and the rider's applied torque on the handlebars aids as well. Bicycles under the proper conditions are so stable that the bike, even absent a rider, can remain upright. This assertion is bolstered by both theory and experiments. Bikes are easy to ride simply because of the favorable physics.

Beginning riders have difficulty staying upright. The rider does not know what to do and thus can't steer correctly. The fearful rider is too rigid and so impedes the bicycle's steering tendencies.

Wide tires and rollers cause the bicycle's physics to be relatively immunized to even unskilled rider commands. Because the trainer bike is so stable, it tends to remain upright even if steering control is incorrectly applied.

Yes, training wheels will allow a bike to remain upright. Unfortunately, a rigid bike denies the learning rider the opportunity to discover that steering actions cause a bike to be balanced. A wide contoured tire with a controlled lateral radius accomplishes three things:

- The mass of the bike and rider is lifted as the bicycle leans.
- The fall rate can be controlled based on what I call lateral contour radius (LCR).
- The learning child is afforded sufficient time to discover balancing by steering.

As such, because the bike and child aren't falling, the child is able to learn. Because falling is largely prevented, the child acts as a stable attractor (to use chaos theory terminology).

I learned many things in my schooling, but I feel compelled to mention one course in particular. As an undergraduate in mechanical engineering at the University of Iowa, I took a required course dealing with fluids and hydraulics. Ships, airplanes, and even bicycles have much in common. They are all subject to roll and therefore have the potential to capsize or fall over. How ships at sea are designed to be stable, thus not rolling over, has a bearing on bicycles as well.

One aspect of the hydraulics course concerned the stability of ships in roll, which is related to what is called the ship's *metacentric height*. When an object tips or rolls, it is stable only if some forces can act to create an opposing or restoring moment. In the case of a ship, the downward action of gravity is one force. A second force is upwards, counter to gravity. This force is the buoyancy action of the water pressing against the ship's hull. This is called the displacement force. Ships are rated in size using the word tonnage.

This refers to the weight of the displaced water; in other words, the upward buoyancy force exerted by the surrounding water acting on the vessel's hull.

When a ship rocks or otherwise has rolled due to steering, wave, or wind action, the shape of the hull combined with the buoyancy or flotation of the displaced water tend to cause a lateral shift in the upward buoyancy force. This lateral shift acts to arrest the roll and bring the vessel back upright. Naval engineers quantify the amount of restoring moment (or torque) based on one measure: the ship's metacentric height.

The metacentric height is defined as the distance between the center of gravity and the vertical projection of the center of buoyancy or flotation. Many dynamic devices such as wheeled vehicles, ships, aircraft, and snow skis are inherently designed to be a compromise pertaining to stability, maneuverability, performance, and the ability to reject disturbances. For example, snow skis for beginners are longer and inherently more stable, but less maneuverable.

Metacentric height is particularly important in ships and other vessels at sea. Ships are designed to meet varied dynamic conditions and requirements.

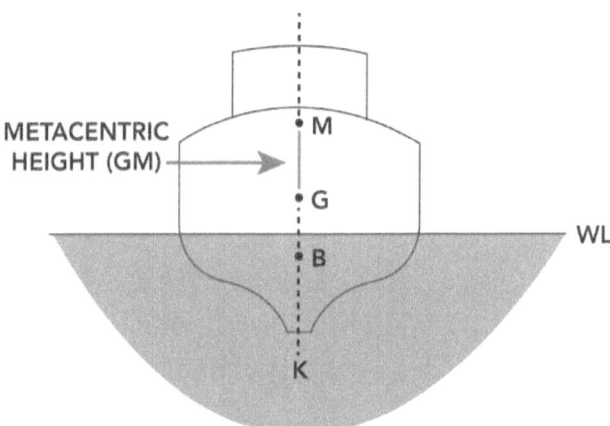

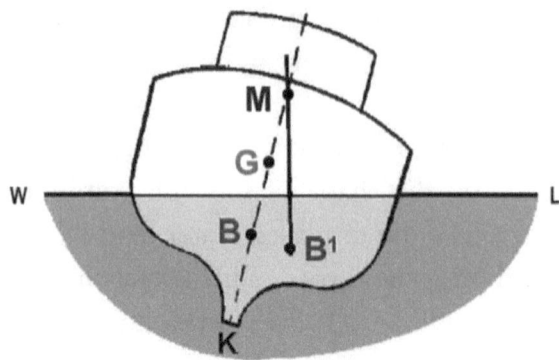

    In the two sketches above, B represents the center of buoyancy (of the displaced water), G represents the center of mass (or center of gravity) of the ship and its cargo, and M represents a mathematical point called the *metacenter*. Now, imagine that the ship has rolled a small angle. Because the hull isn't round like a cylinder or a log, the center of buoyancy (B) shifts in the direction of the roll. One then draws a vertical line upward from the center of buoyancy (B) until one intersects the centerline of the ship.

    In this situation, it is assumed that the sea is calm (absence of wave action) and that the ship is symmetric in cross-section. The distance between M and G is the metacentric height. The restoring moment for a ship when it is rolling is the product of the ship's displacement times the horizontal distance between the two respective vertical forces (shown in the second diagram as arrows or vectors). The restoring moment acts to reverse the rolling or capsizing action. Note in the figure above that the upward force of the buoyancy has shifted in the direction of roll (to the right) of the downward gravity force. These two forces are not aligned but rather offset with respect to each other. When two equal and yet opposite forces act, but are not aligned, a twisting action on the floating ship results. This twisting action is what is called the *restoring moment*.

    It would appear at first glance that flat vessels, like barges, are more stable than ships with hulls that are more rounded in cross-section. While true, the problem is that, in addition to stability, ships at sea must also be seaworthy. Wave action will adversely toss and upset flat vessels, like river barges, so the design of an ocean-going ship must necessarily be based on a compromise between stability and wave rejection.

If we apply these shaping principles to the roller bike, the conclusion is that rollers do wonders for the learning child as long as the riding surface is both flat and hard. That's why the adaptive bike program uses the roller bikes in gymnasiums and on other hard-surfaced areas as these adaptive bikes would function poorly on uneven surfaces. Maneuverability and disturbance rejection are not important design attributes. Our goal is to get the novice rider to master balance skills.

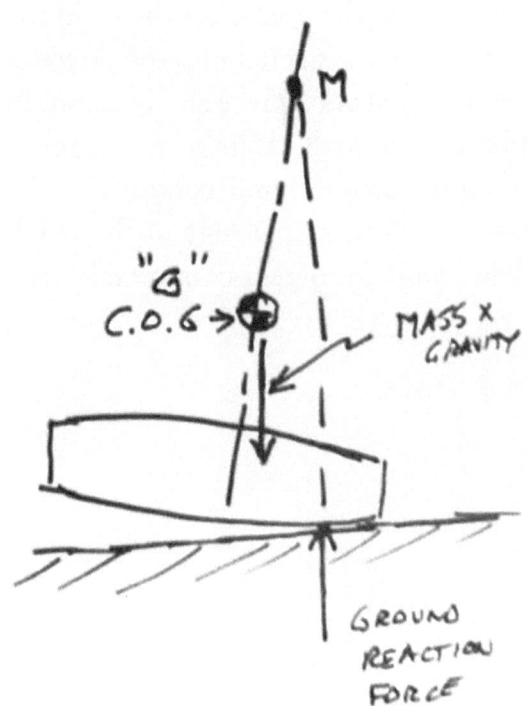

When we use a wide tire or roller on a bike, we are able to dictate the metacentric height. The roll or tip of a bike with rider can be controlled based on the distance between the height of the center of gravity of the bike and the vertical projection of the support point where the roller (or tire) contacts the ground.

There are strong similarities as we consider ships and roller bicycles. The metacentric height varies per the shape of the hull or, in the case of roller bikes, to the lateral contour of the roller. When the metacentric height goes to zero, the ship is no longer stable. Conventional bikes with narrow tires have a negative metacentric height. Consequently, without steering or some other means of correction, the bike will capsize.

The purpose of the roller in the trainer bike design is to cause the metacentric height of the bicycle to be positive. That way, the trainer bike with an appropriately contoured roller will not fall over even if the bike isn't moving. As the child pedals and experiments with steering, the goal is for the child to discover that the bike behaves better when steered into the direction of fall. The trainer with the roller works precisely because the child can experiment without constantly falling over. Also, in the bike program I have rollers with varying contours. This allows us to gradually increase the level of challenge as the child improves in his or her skills and becomes comfortable in the biking environment.

A NOTE FROM THE AUTHOR

Dear Reader,

Thank you for taking the time to read *The Bike Whisperer*. As an 80-something-year-old retired professor, I'm making it a priority to chronicle aspects of my past that I find notable and noteworthy so that I can leave a legacy for readers like you for years to come. This book is just one of such books and I'm happy to have been able to share it with you.

I hope you enjoyed *The Bike Whisperer*. If so, I'd appreciate if you left a review on Amazon. Reviews help other readers decide to try out a new book. Just a sentence or two saying what you liked about the book will do!

Thanks again for reading and for helping get my books into the hands of other readers.

Blessings,
Richard E. Klein

MORE TITLES FROM RICHARD E. KLEIN

Dumb Dickie: A Memoir of Learning, Growth, Hope, and Blunders

Kisses When I Get Home: Letters of a Long-Distance Courtship During World War II

Circling the Drain: Humorous Musings on Becoming a Mechanical Engineer

The Deadly Gamble: A Post-Mortem of the World Trade Center Collapse

Second Dissertation Upon Roast Pig: Practicalities and Philosophies for the 21st Century

Bikes Are Big on Planet Klynia (A Children's Book)

We're All Set: Selected Klein Family Memories

ABOUT THE AUTHOR

Richard E. Klein earned his Ph.D. in engineering from Purdue University in 1969 and taught systems theory for three decades at the University of Illinois in Urbana-Champaign before retiring in 1998. He holds a particular interest in bicycle stability and control, and has devoted much of his time and energy to developing a national program for teaching children with disabilities to master bike riding. Visit iCanBike.org and RainbowTrainers.com for more info.

By his own admission, Dr. Klein is an incurable romantic and altruist. His writings and musings are filled with hope and bright horizons despite having lived through World War II and the Korean War as a child, both of which deeply impacted his worldview. Through his books, he aims to point the way towards a better internal mindset and a better world.

Richard and his wife of more than 50 years, Marjorie Maxwell Klein, reside in the St. Louis area. They have two children and six grandchildren. Richard writes for them and for generations to come.

ACKNOWLEDGEMENTS

The development of this bike program required many hands and many minds. I have never been alone in my endeavors. Those responsible for the development of the biking program are (and were) much like a marching column. Some joined the column in progress. Some dropped out. Some even died. Some were born. Nonetheless, the column continued to move forward. The column has never stopped and will not ever stop. I express my deep appreciation and thanks to all who have assisted along the way. The numbers go into the hundreds and thousands. Any attempt to list their names would contribute little. Those who pitched in already know who they are and know of their priceless contributions.

I do wish to acknowledge certain teachers and mentors: Marian (Mary) Olha (my 7th and 8th grade science teacher at Wilcoxson Grade School in Stratford, Connecticut), Dr. Donald Olson (Pennsylvania State University), Professor Arthur D. Brickman (my MS thesis advisor at Penn State), Dr. Robert H. Kohr (Purdue University), Dr. R. E. "Gene" Goodson (my PhD dissertation advisor at Purdue University), and Walter Kaufmann (aeronautical engineer at Hughes Aircraft Company, Missile Systems Division, Canoga Park, California). Acknowledgement is given to Dr. Douglas L. Marriott because he had such a unique way of succinctly expressing matters. For example, I attribute the phrase "Build it wrong, but build it" to Doug.

Special thanks go to my best friend and devoted companion in life, my wife Marjorie.

REFERENCES

1. Klein, R. E., *The Deadly Gamble: A Post-Mortem of the World Trade Center Collapse*, Independently Published, (available from www.amazon.com), 2019.

2. Blumenfeld, R.D., *In the Days of Bicycles and Bustles*, Brewer and Warren Inc., New York, 1930, p. 20.

3. Kuo, B. C., *Automatic Control Systems*, Prentice-Hall, Englewood Cliffs, New Jersey, 1961.

4. Klein, R.E., "Bang-Bang Control Optimization of Ignition Timing in an Internal Combustion Engine," *M.S. Thesis in Mechanical Engineering*, Pennsylvania State University, 1965.

5. Bloom, B. S. (Editor), *Taxonomy of Educational Objectives*, David McKay Company, New York, 1956.

6. Hand, R. S., *Comparisons and Stability Analysis of Linearized Equations for a Basic Bicycle Model*, M.S. Thesis, Department of Theoretical and Applied Mechanics, Cornell University, New York, 1988.

7. Jones, David, "The Stability of the Bicycle," *Physics Today*, 1970, April 1, pp. 34-40.

8. Scholl, R., *et al.* (1974). United States Patent No. *3,795,285*. United States Patent.

9. Roland, R. D., "Computer simulation of bicycle dynamics," *Mechanics and Sport* (AMD-4, ed. J. L. Bleustein), pp. 35–83. New York: American Society of Mechanical Engineers, 1973.

10. Andrews, Travis M., "106 million people watched 'M.A.S.H.' finale 35 years ago. No scripted show since has come close," *Washington Post*, 28 February 2018.

<https://www.washingtonpost.com/news/morning-mix/wp/2018/02/28/106-million-people-watched-mash-finale-35-years-ago-no-scripted-show-has-come-close-since/>

11. Astrom, K. J., R. E. Klein, and A. Lennartsson, "Bicycle Dynamics and Control," *IEEE Control Systems Magazine,* Institute of Electrical & Electronic Engineers (IEEE), August 2005.

12. Klein, R. E., *Bikes Are Big on Planet Klynia,* Independently Published, (available from www.amazon.com), 2020.

13. *ASME NEWS*, Vol. 8, No. 2, June 1988.

14. Klein, R. E., "Novel Systems and Dynamics Teaching Techniques Using Bicycles," *Proceedings of the 1988 American Control Conference*, Atlanta GA, pp. 1157-1160, June 15-17, 1988.

15. Klein, R. E., "Using Bicycles to Teach Systems Dynamics," *IEEE Control Systems Magazine*, April 1989, pp. 4-9.

16. Truxal, J.G., *Automatic Feedback Control Systems Synthesis*, McGraw-Hill, New York, 1955.

17. Evans, W. R., *Control Systems Dynamics*, McGraw-Hill, New York, 1954.

18. Klein, R. E., "Teaching Linear Systems Theory Using Cramer's Rule," *IEEE Transactions on Engineering Education*, Vol. 33, No. 3, August 1990, pp. 258-267.

19. Klein, R. E., "The University of Illinois Bicycle Project," *International Federation of Automatic Control*, Boston MA, June 1991.

20. Klein, R. E. "How Children Learn to Ride," *The Rivendell Reader*, Vol. 1, No. 3. 1993, p. 15.

21. Cudmore, P. (1974). United States Patent No. *US3794351A*. United States Patent.

22. Klein, R. E., "Design and Use of Adapted Training Bicycles for Children With Special Needs," NAFAPA Symposium, Minneapolis MN, October 1998.

23. Klein, R. E., P. DiRocco, B. Oberweiser, M. Mallett, R. Heath,

"Adapted Bicycling Taught Using a Camp Format," California Adapted Physical Education Symposium, San Diego CA, October 1999.

24. DiRocco, P., R. Klein, "The UW–L Bike Camp: A Bicycling Camp for Exceptional Children," California Adapted Physical Education and Dance Conference, Fresno CA, October 2000.

25. DiRocco, P., R. Klein, "Adapted Bicycling and Dynamical Systems," International Adapted Physical Education Symposium, Vienna, July 2001.

26. Featured in *Midwest Living* magazine, Nov/Dec 2004, p. 14.

27. "Rollers and the Renaissance Man," *Illinois Alumni,* March/April 2004, p. 10.

28. Ulrich, D. *et al*, "A Bicycle Training Intervention" University of Michigan, NCT02046889. ClinicalTrials.gov, 2013.

29. *Bicycling Magazine,* Vol. XLVI, No. 11, December 2005.

30. Klein, R. E., "Build It Wrong, But Build It: A Bicycle Trek," Bicycle and Motorcycle Dynamics Symposium, Delft, The Netherlands, 2010

31. Pontryagin, L. S.; Boltyanskii, V. G.; Gamkrelidze, R. V.; Mishchenko, E. F. (1962). "The Mathematical Theory of Optimal Processes." English translation. Interscience. *ISBN 2-88124-077-1.*